1

Contextualization: More Than a Missiological Methodology

Introduction

Perhaps this world is not yet a global village, as McLuhan would have us believe, but "universal" changes are happening. And the biggest change is "change" itself. Most likely there is not a village in the world that has not heard an airplane overhead. Economic structure and rhythms ebb and flow in direct relation to the operation of the major money markets. Price fluctuations in Europe even determine the number of villagers in northern Nigeria who will be hired when they migrate south to the plantations.

Shoki Coe, writing in *Theological Education*, described what is now happening to various degrees in every culture: ". . . the most important factor, especially since the last war, has been the new phenomenon of radical change. The new context is not that of static culture, but the search for the new, which at the same time has involved the culture itself."(1) The Christian church must be aware of this rapid change in the various cultures worldwide.

It has often been observed that uprooted people are very open to the gospel message. Traditional mores are radically affected by the pressure of new demands and new, or rearranged, resources. Values come under inspection as old patterns of belief and practice are called upon to help the displaced person cope with his new environment. If the old ways fail him at this point, he is open to something new, or at least something new to him, that will help him to cope with his new situation.

In a sense the whole world, in larger and smaller groupings, is being uprooted by forces such as war, famine, oppression, secularization, urbanization, and nationalism. In
these new contexts people are looking for answers specially
suited to their current needs. When modern man turns to
Christianity he expects it to help him to cope with the problems of the times. If he obtains little or no aid, he often discards it. One of the reasons for rejection has been
suggested by Agbeti: ". . . it is not religion or Christianity *per se* that people tend to oppose in Africa, but the
foreignness of the Christian approach to evangelism and
vital national issues." (2) It is not so much a matter of
seeing or not seeing the relevance of Christianity in a new
setting. What often is needed in the new context is to
really *see* Christianity. Charles R. Taber writes that if
Christianity is not appropriated to/for the context, true
Christianity is not possible. The religion found instead
"will either be an unthinking conformity to external rules,
which is the heresy of legalism, or a pretense of conformity,
which is hypocrisy." He then reacts to the scope of the
problem: "I am afraid both of these problems are rampant in
various parts of the world."(3)

Legalism and hypocrisy as mentioned by Taber are often
the problem of Christians who have no other choice. Many
are not instructed enough in the truths of the Christian
faith to be able to rise above such problems. They find
that their faith has various lacunae when it comes to every-
day implementation of their faith. It is true that the Holy
Spirit worked in the lives of the disciples to teach them
all things.(4) Yet, Christ also instructed his followers
to make disciples, teaching new believers to observe all
that Christ commanded.(5)

It has been reported that in at least one instance in
Kenya a woman is scornful of Christianity because those in
the local Christian congregation are influenced hardly at
all by Christianity in their daily lives. Much of the problem in this has been specifically imputed to the lack
of teaching and relevant application received by the mostly
illiterate congregation.(6) Thus, the problem can be two-
fold, not enough teaching and not enough of the right kind
of teaching of the way of Christ.

Before the turn of this century the "three-self" approach
was developed to provide a way of encouraging new local
congregations to stand on their own, apart from the aid of
their sponsoring churches.(7) Proponents of this approach

advocated the planting of congregations that were self-supporting, self-governing, and self-propagating. Such churches were successful, to varying degrees, in standing alone apart from the parent churches. Most of the official theology of these newly-planted churches, however, was largely the imported theology, foreign in structure and application.

Very few local works on theology were written, largely due to the fact that writing was not the principal method of communication in these cultures. No doubt, some theologizing and reformulating was done. Kosuke Koyama has described this as "salt and pepper theology."(8) But on the whole, imported Christianity was the only Christianity the people ever knew in their relatively static cultures, although many undoubtedly sensed the need for something deeper.

Today, that "something deeper" is being sought with two emphases in mind. The first is in evangelism. What is relevant to the unsaved modern heart? The second concerns how to live as a Christian. Various practical areas that need to become nationalized or ethnicized, have been discerned within these two major emphases. In his booklet *Towards an Indigenous Church*, E. Bolaji Idowu lists these areas: modes of worship, hymnody, prayer, the Scriptures, evangelistic terminology, preaching style, liturgy, dress and vestments, quotations and theology.(9)

Three major groups in Christianity are struggling with these questions. The three groups, roughly delineated, are: 1) the Roman Catholic church, 2) the ecumenical or conciliar movement, which includes the Orthodox churches, the so-called mainline Protestant churches, and those in the Third World churches who hold to higher critical views of the Scriptures and advocate liberal theologies, and 3) the conservative evangelical churches(10) around the world and their related missionary sending agencies, who, basically, hold to the inerrancy of the Bible and interpret it in its natural sense.(11)

Only a passing reference can be given to the Roman church in this book. However, many parallels exist theologically and ecclesiologically between the ecumenical churches and the Roman church.

The Ecumenical Approach to Dealing with the World

This group's basic approach in recent years has come to be termed "contextualization." Contextualization was proposed as a missiological methodology and carried with it a lot of implied theology, which was part of the conciliar scene. Apparently the desire was to make all aspects of Christianity relevant to every ethnic group, or even to formulate a new Christianity which would be relevant. Cultural relativism, a nondescript yet pervasive belief that has been widely held since World War II,(12) has been a part of the thinking involved in contextualism. Each culture was seen in a positive light as being able to contribute elements to the local Christian thought and practice. Some of these elements were considered worthy of export to the Christian church in other cultures.

Some missionaries working prior to World War II, and even afterward, seemed to consider only the sending culture; or perhaps it would be more appropriate to say that they assumed it to be *the* correct culture. Elements of the sending culture were presented as being an integral part of the gospel. These cultural accretions received mixed reaction from those on whom they were being imposed.

Meanwhile, Europe was entering into a post-Christian era, of sorts. Social structures relating to religion were still maintained, but the spiritual life was lacking. Liberal European theologians frustrated with the state of affairs were ready to clean house. Thus, they were more than ready to dispense with the very cultural elements that missionaries had been exporting. A type of guilt reaction arose facilitating interest in change. Thus there was a doubly important need to search for ways to make a seemingly deformed, or irrelevant Christianity relevant to the lives of every people in every context.(13)

The term "contextualization" first surfaced publicly in 1972 with the publication of *Ministry in Context* by the Theological Education Fund (TEF).(14) In the book, four areas were targeted for contextualization efforts: missiology, educational structures, theology, and pedagogy. (15)

Ministry in Context was the working policy of the third mandate for the TEF. It was developed to guide implementation of that mandate, which was to cover the period 1970 to 1977. The first two mandates had the emphases of "advance" and "rethink."(16) The third mandate directed a more radical

break from the first mandate than did the second. TEF was
moving in a new direction. Its emphasis was now on *reform*
of the old ways of doing things.

A radical change in direction for the missionary program
of the World Council of Churches (WCC) and related organizations had been foretold by many critics of the merger of the
International Missionary Conference (IMC) and the WCC.
Twelve years after the 1960 merger, movement towards a radical change was becoming evident.(17) Whether this change
was to be significant or not, and the final extent of the
changes, was not apparent to most observers.

The working policy read, in part: ". . . to help the
churches *reform* [emphasis mine] the training for the Christian ministry. . . by providing selective and temporary
assistance and consultative services to institutions for
theological education and other centres of training."(18)
There was to be punch in the TEF's proclamation. TEF was
to regulate its millions of dollars for grants directly in
relation to how well each applicant for funds contextualized
its missiology, theology, structures and pedagogy.

In order to more clearly understand the four-fold thrust
of contextualization as defined by the TEF in 1972, some
background material must be presented. Worthy of note will
be any presuppositions and/or methodologies that were inherent in TEF's use of the term.

The Background to Conciliar Contextualization

In 1971 a consultation on "Dogmatic or Contextual Theology?" was held by the Ecumenical Institute of the WCC at
Bossey, Switzerland. Dr. Nikos A. Nissiotis of the Orthodox
Church, then director of the Ecumenical Institute and chairman of the consultation, sent out a circular letter in advance of the session. Dated October 1970 it read in part:

> We consider the study of this question
> "Dogmatic or Contextual Theology?" to be
> necessary at the present time on account
> of the crisis which has arisen through the
> continued use of abstract principles and
> metaphysical presuppositions by some theo-
> retical disciplines. It is evident that,
> in the realm of theology, this crisis would
> affect Systematic Theology more than any
> other discipline. And Systematic Theology

has indeed been largely affected by the
changes which, due to the rise of a new
technological society, have taken place
in the world. The effect of the latter
has been to lead to a kind of "contextual
or experiential" theology which gives
preference, as the point of departure
for systematic theological thinking to
the contemporary historical scene *over
against the biblical tradition* [emphasis
mine] and confessional statements constructed on the basis of biblical texts,
taken as a whole and thus used uncriti-
cally. At the same time the question is
being raised today of whether Systematic
Theology can continue to take biblical
texts as its point of departure and, on
the basis of Biblical Theology, systematize the Christian Faith.(19)

The consultation met in August of 1971. The group appeared to envision a radical reevaluation of much of the
theology then being espoused, especially in conciliar circles. This new evaluation was to be a critical part in the
reform that the third mandate hoped to encourage. The consultation was unsure of its footing as it proceeded, as evidenced by the seeming lack of consensus during the discussions.

The modern world and its problems and insights loomed
large before the participants. They were committed to analyzing the world to which Christianity should be relevant.(20)
Sighting in on specific instances in local contexts, they
advocated what might be called a theology of fragments.(21)
These fragments were welcomed as highly relevant revelations
of God's will--relevant supplements to dogmatic theology as
the group saw it.(22) Contextualized theology and dogmatic
pronouncements were expected to inform each other, and to
engage in dialogue. Nissiotis introduced the report on the
results of the finished conference partly as follows:

In other words, we wanted to raise the question of whether theology today can be conceived either as an esoteric, self-sufficient
science based on its own premises alone or
whether these *premises* must also be sought
in the experimental realm of thought and
action of the *environment* [emphasis mine] of

>   which theology is a part and for which it
>   exists.(23)

Thus, contextualized theology was seen as existing for its
environment and as experimentally derived from it. This derived contextual theology saw much of a positive nature in
the local culture. The world was seen as God's world,(24)
and although evil might be found, good things were to be
hoped for and experienced in the future.(25)

A double premise came to be seen as the basis for a total
theological position. Balance between the two was to be derived in "a continuous tension allowing for a reciprocal
criticism which warns against any one-sided emphasis placed
on one of these elements."(26)

Both sources, or premises, of theology were considered in
some sense relative. Cultures, of course, were constantly
changing. The context of modern man constantly was being
changed by new influences. An earlier consultation at
Bossey had been held on the topic of rapid culture change.
It was determined that this had caused, in part, "the crisis"
of the European church of the sixties and early seventies.
(27) It was decided that European Christianity was not
relevant even in Europe, because it did not speak to the
ever-changing European.

Dogmatic theology was seen as a relative source because
modern European theologies were changing. Liberalism had
been supplanted by, or at least supplemented by, Barthian
thought. Bultmann and Tillich modified theology into their
own patterns. The Roman Catholic magisterium was no longer
the unquestioned fountainhead of relevant interpretations.
Higher criticism continued to make even the Bible and its
teachings less than certain.(28)

Although a theological dialectical interaction between
contextual and dogmatic theology was expected to be the
method of the future, any synthesis of the two seemed likely
to place greatest emphasis on the context. Nissiotis' summary, quoted above, revealed a basic distrust of the Bible
as a source for Systematic Theology: "The question is being
raised today of whether Systematic Theology can continue to
take biblical texts as its point of departure and, on the
basis of Biblical Theology, systematize the Christian
Faith."(29)

Apparently Nissiotis' unhappiness was with Biblical Theology as a specific theological school of thought. Whether he could have retained an authoritative use of the Bible as a premise, while jettisoning Biblical Theology, seemingly, was not considered.

In the consultation, another who downplayed the Systematic-Biblical branch of theology was A. O. Dyson. His paper, which was an integral part of the discussion, was negative in its critique of the "diremptive," or fragmenting, nature of modern dogmatic theology. He described dogmatic theology as appealing to "words" such as "revelation," "Bible," "Scripture and tradition." His critique was of modern and confessional use of such sources.(30)

Contextual theology was seen as a balance to, if not the replacement for, the modern theologies of Europe. To be sure, some, such as Harvey Cox, had done much research in the current scene. Yet he and others had left themselves open to the charge of writing only biblical-exegetical foot-notes to secular paragraphs.(31) The consultation wanted more.

The concepts that developed in the meeting and in later practice might be graphed as in figures 1 and 2. The two partners, dogmatic theology and contextual theology, were to interact with each other, to inform each other and to in-spire and foster a relevant Christianity for the seventies.

Dogmatics, said to be past-centered, was seen as based on a mixture of methods and themes. Most important of these were higher criticism and its accompanying hermeneutics, and the theological method of focusing on only certain biblical themes at the expense of others. Several of the key themes emphasized were "disclosure," "kerygma," "word-event" and "sitz im lieben."(32) The tendency of over-selectivity in dogmatics was seen by some as a tendency possible to con-textual theology as well. It was hoped, however, that any diremptive tendencies would be balanced by use of a frame-work of major philosophical and theological motifs, such as early Marxism, and the Exodus and Incarnation motifs. Con-textualized fragments in framework hopefully would escape what was seen as the "synthetic" nature of dogmatic theology, and would appear rather as a well-ordered mosaic.(33)

An example of a contextualized theological fragment which then would be related to a framework of some kind can now be given. Let us envision a group of Christians trying

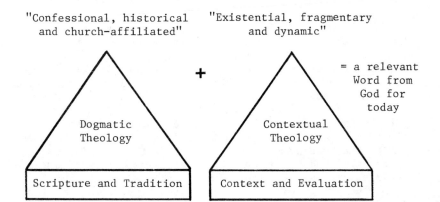

"Confessional, historical and church-affiliated"   "Existential, fragmentary and dynamic"

Dogmatic Theology   +   Contextual Theology   = a relevant Word from God for today

Scripture and Tradition   Context and Evaluation

Figure 1:   The double premise

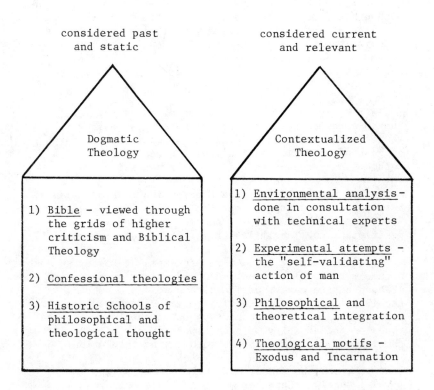

considered past and static   considered current and relevant

Dogmatic Theology   Contextualized Theology

1) Bible - viewed through the grids of higher criticism and Biblical Theology

2) Confessional theologies

3) Historic Schools of philosophical and theological thought

1) Environmental analysis- done in consultation with technical experts

2) Experimental attempts - the "self-validating" action of man

3) Philosophical and theoretical integration

4) Theological motifs - Exodus and Incarnation

Figure 2:   A closer inspection of the theological base of each type of theology as seen at Boosey.

to decide whether or not a cross-town expressway should be
built in Chicago. The questions are whether or not, where,
and how to build the highway. They realize that they are
not sufficiently informed to make the right choice. Techni-
cians in the field of road building, experts in displacement
of communities, and politicians are consulted in a series
of meetings, along with local merchants and residents. In
such a "Christian context," namely as Christians evaluate
the situation, a Christian opinion is developed on the matter of the crosstown highway. The result is considered a
"word" from God on the matter. It will be a Word from God,
mediated by the Christian community related to a specific
situation. This could be called a theology of roadbuilding.
It is only a theological fragment but can be integrated with
other fragments by being fitted into a larger philosophical
whole.

The approach illustrated has not been without precedent,
although the terminology and some of the theological under-
pinnings are new. The extremely radical Ecumenical Institute in Evanston, Illinois, and the Ecumenical Institute
in Bossey, Switzerland, have advocated such secular-
Christian interplay for years. They have actively sought
advice on which programs to implement or endorse.

In a study session on rapid social change and the
Church's relation to it, a panel member discussing the
topic "Bible Study on finding the will of God" ventured the
suggestion that finding God's will comes best by a new
method: prayer and the opinion of experts.(34)

One of those who attended the session reacted somewhat
bitterly to such suggestions and to the whole process:
". . . it's like a group of pseudo-sociologists, quasi-
politicians and facsimiles of marketing researchers."(35)

With the passage of time the attempts at Bossey no doubt
became more sophisticated. And the weight of authority
granted to the expert advice became more pronounced. At
the 1971 conference on theology, Dyson advocated consultation with experts when contextualizing theology and also
revealed the affinity of such a methodology with political
theologies; in this case the theology of revolution.

> . . . the *contextual approach* has an in-
> ductive character which should encourage
> fraternal relations with the empiricist
> approach in the human and natural sciences.

On this scheme a "theology of revolution"
is not deduced from an overall theological framework. The process rather begins
with a technical understanding of the
particular revolutionary situation, which
is *later connected with certain theological motifs* [emphasis mine]. Contextualism's concern for facts inevitably exposes
theology to a wide range of contentious
argument among the secular experts as to
what the facts are and as to what kinds
of value they bear. We shall have to ask
what kind of difference the introduction
of theological motifs could make to a conclusion based on complex and often technical evidence.(36)

Two things must be noted in Dyson's words. First he
talked of relating the results of empiricist approach in
the human and natural sciences to theological motifs selected *after* the research findings were in. Secondly, he
closely related, if not identified, the methodology of a
contextual approach with that of political theology.(37)

Orthopraxis, or right practice, had been stressed heavily
in the political theologies. The "doing" of theology appeared virtually identical to the pragmatic emphasis in
contextual theologizing.(38)

At the consultation various small groups were formed for
discussion among the thirty or so present. Various formulations on the title "Dogmatic or Contextual Theology?"
were proposed. The list given below is representative of
much of the discussion and the basic differences seen between dogmatic and contextual theology. (1) On point of
departure, dogmatic theology moves from the revelation of
God to the modern world. Contextual theology moves from
the modern situation to revelation. (2) On a general to
individual continuum, dogmatic theology is considered uni-
versally valid. It deals in basic principles and it has an
open framework. Contextual theology deals with analysis of
a particular situation. (3) On time concepts, dogmatic
theology considers the whole of time. Contextual theology
concentrates on the present. (4) On a continuum between
ontological and functional, dogmatic theology deals epistemo-
logically with knowledge or being. Contextual theology
deals functually with being. (5) On unity versus plurality,
dogmatic theology underlines unity. Contextual theology

underlines plurality. (6) On the receptive-active continuum, dogmatic theology affirms the action of God with man
as being receptive. Contextual theology emphasizes the
creative and the self-affirming action of men. (7) Considering the deductive vs. inductive approach, dogmatic
theology is deductive and addressed to the church. Contextual theology is more inductive and related to the world.
(39)

2

The Theological Context: Political Theology

Before any further discussion is made of the actual guidelines which were laid down for those who were going to contextualize in accord with the TEF,(1) the theological scene
of the times must be considered briefly. Secular and political theologies were on the scene and influenced those who
formulated the basic guidelines for contextualization.

Alistair Kee, in *A Reader in Political Theology*, attempted
to trace an evolution of political theologies in the sixties.
He began with a section on "The Christian-Marxist Dialogue"
and then moved to "The Theology of Hope," "The Theology of
Liberation" and "Black Theology." He ended his book with
sections on "Violence" and "Christian Resistance."(2) The
following comments on the theologies of the sixties will
follow his outline. Appropriate references will be drawn
from primary works and evaluative discussions.

At first glance it becomes obvious that the evolutionary
scheme presented by Kee, tracing the movement of one theological school into another, is not clear-cut. Black theologians did not wait for the findings of theologians of liberation to become evident before starting their works. Yet
the basic outline in Kee's work provides a good framework
for discussion.

During the sixties many side currents, and other significant contemporary and earlier works, were influencing theological thought. Process theology advocated by Whitehead,
Hartshorne and Cobb must be mentioned.(3) Roman Catholic

theology, developing along new lines during this time, was
involved in dialogue with the contemporary issues and with
non-Catholic theologians.(4)

Despite its errors, the following quote from *Newsweek*
(April, 1977) provides a good picture of the mix between
Protestant and Roman Catholic thought.

> Increasingly . . . the Roman Catholic and Pro-
> testant churches are responding to a new
> "liberation theology" that came out of
> Vatican II in the '60's and is now espoused
> by the World Council of Churches. Geared
> to ministering to the "whole man"--body and
> soul--liberation theology contends that faith
> must be manifested in concrete terms. "We
> want to free man from all that is sin, whe-
> ther it is undernourishment, illiteracy, or
> oppression," says Maryknoll priest Larry
> Egan.(5)

Liberation theology was not only rooted in Vatican II as
will be outlined below,(6) but it became a trans-ecclesiastical
phenomenon. A common criticism points out priest Egan's
selective use of "horizontal" sins: "undernourishment, il-
literacy or oppression." His omission of sins such as idol-
atry, apostasy and blasphemy, more "vertical" in nature, reflected deep theological roots.

Hopeful Theologizing

> Those who hope in Christ can no longer put
> up with reality as it is, but begin to suf-
> fer under it, to contradict it. Peace with
> God means conflict with the world. . .(7)

Jürgen Moltmann, quoted above, who published in the early
1960's his *Theologie der Hoffnung* which made its debut in
1967 in English as *The Theology of Hope*, is the major theologian of "hope." Using the words "hope" and "eschatology"
as his major themes, Moltmann invests them with a meaning
substantially different from both traditional and liberal
usages.

Apparently, Moltmann was dislodged from his satisfied
assent to Barthianism when he read the work of the Dutch
Catholic, Arnold von Ruler. Soon after, he read the neo-
Marxist Jewish philosopher Ernst Bloch on the hope principle.

Herein he found integration of his concerns for mission and
the kingdom of God with his views of the Old and New Testa-
ments as presented by von Rad and Kasemann.(8) Moltmann,
however, did more than restore eschatology to its rightful
place in theology. He made it the key to understanding all
theology.(9)

> From first to last, and not merely in the
> epilogue, Christianity is eschatology, is
> hope, forward looking and forward moving,
> and therefore also revolutionizing and trans-
> forming the present. The eschatological
> is not one element of Christianity, but it
> is the medium of Christian faith as such,
> the key in which everything in it is set. . .(10)

To Moltmann a hope which was substantial was an option
which could be brought to pass. And if it could be brought
to pass, men should move to bring it to pass. Moltmann invested much thought in the area of eschatology and history.
He assailed what he considered the Greek concept of history
where God is viewed as the transcendent Other who is above
or beyond the process of the world, and who reveals himself
in recurring epiphanies of eternal presence.(11)

Modern historiography and modern philosophy were seen as
promoting "a subliminal annihilation of history."(12) For
one thing, objective analysis of past trends seemed to Moltmann to kill the liveliness, or the open options, that existed in the past presents. To label things seemed to ignore
the fact that *this* present is only a part of the process of
time which could not be properly evaluated until the culmination of all time.

To compound the problem, Moltmann saw around him a decay-
ing non-eschatological, bourgeois Christianity in a post-
Christian Europe.(13) Society had developed slots and pock-
ets into which the decrepit church had crept. Because man
in his technological world had been stereotyped into regular
molds while on the job, modern man was seeking subjective
freedoms for himself that would be his prerogative and his
alone. One of these deep-inside, private affairs was religion as the cult of subjectivity, which said, "My religion
is a *private*, personal affair, and can be fully experienced
as such."

To meet social needs in a society of stereotypes, volun-
tary associations sprang up. The church in Europe as "the

cult of co-humanity" evolved into one such association. Religious experts came to fill a required place in a secular
world. If they did their job well, it was blithely supposed
that others need not worry about spiritual matters. As
Moltmann saw it, these experts and their systems became society's cult of the institution.(14) And against this Christianity he reacted.

     Moltmann stressed "the new factor."(15) Always emphasiz-
ing open options, he presented his view:

               An eschatology of history. . . which re-
               volves around the concepts of the new and
               the future, of mission and the front line
               of the present, would be in a position to
               take history as history, to remember and
               expect it as history, and thus not to anni-
               hilate history but to keep it open.(16)

     As man encountered these options, Moltmann believed he
would be invigorated and would try to change things. "This
horizon [the future] fills him with hopeful expectation and
at the same time requires of him responsibility and decision
for the world of history."(17) Moltmann described God's
task as making these possibilities possible. The task of
man, then, was to see the possibilities and to work toward
them. Thus, as man took one option, God was to reveal another, and another, into which man then would struggle. God
was described as faithful in his work, which was to "create
real, objective possibilities for his mission." Man's job
was "a certain *Weltenschauung*, a confidence in the world and
a hope for the world."(18)

     New options were assumed by Moltmann to be good options
or at least it was to be assumed that most good options
might be carried out. Moltmann spoke of ". . . a faith in
the great task of mankind." ". . . the summons to the eschatological hope of final and universal salvation." ". . .
being on the way to true humanity, to that which is appointed
for all man." "Hoping in the promised new creation by God
. . ." ". . . the world . . . is a vast container full of
future and of boundless possibilities for good and for evil.
(19)

     Transcendence, as such, was virtually absent in Moltmann's
system. Man was to choose and act. Doctrinal statements
were validated only as they proved to agree with an existing
reality that moved forward into the open opportunities.(20)

Sin and death were seen as realities of the present,
bounds which were to be crossed and transcended even as
Christ on the cross and by his resurrection went beyond the
power and restraints of sin and death. It must be noted that
these concepts did not imply imputation of and/or propitia-
tion of sin before a righteous and wrathful Judge. Rather
the resurrection was to help man gain "an open prospect in
which there is nothing more to oppress us, a view of the
realm of freedom and of joy."(21)

Quoting Kierkegaard, Moltmann developed his theology of
hope along lines which easily stimulated political and social action: ". . . hope becomes a passion for what is possible. . . because it can be a passion for what has been made
possible. . . this future of openness and freedom in the
Christ event."(22)

Moltmann's position on active participation in life became exceedingly important as his thoughts became translated
into political theory. This easily happened as Moltmann not
only advocated "Christian" interaction on the personal level
but also in the *structures* of society. This was to result
in a general Christian restructuring of things:

> The concrete humanity disclosed by the
> Christian mission must therefore enter
> into debate with the universal defini-
> tions of humanity in philosophic anthro-
> pology, and for its part also outline
> general structures of human nature, in
> which the future of faith shines as a
> foreglow of the future of all men.(23)

Moltmann repudiated existentialism's obsession with the non-
historical present, and historical views that lacked an
"open" view of the future. Congruent to such a position, he
derived a system that was antagonistic toward any views of
special revelation from God. History was seen as one piece,
to be evaluated from one point only, the future. "Every-
thing is caught up in time, or flux, and moves along in a
universe of one essential level of dimension."(24) The
"God who calls and promises" was seen as revealing himself
in the event of promise.(25) As God was with Jeremiah, so
he was seen as interacting with contemporary man.(26)

To this present-centered revelation, which looked ever
forward, Moltmann added insights from the world or its contexts. The Christian mission was seen as having concrete

form. This meant that there were choices and actions boldly
made in the secular-political world. Hopeful action even
implied a Christian anthropology which was willing to "outline general structures of human nature." That more
"Christian"-like structures could be implemented was to be
guaranteed by the very nature of Moltmann's God.(27)

Along with Moltmann, others were struggling to make sense
of revelation as they perceived it in today's world. A ren-
aissance of the teachings of the young Marx laid stress on
praxis. It seemed very clear that philosophers and theologians could not expect to reach a correct interpretation of
the world unless they became involved in an ongoing process
of engaging with the world.(28) Those who refused to come
out of their ivory towers were dismissed as mere theoreti-
cians of a world of history-less non-realities, subtle spin-
ners of non-substantial systems.

In 1968 Moltmann entered the dispute in the French students' demonstration. The time was ripe for commitment.
Rapid change was the order of the day and, much like Mao's
"continuing revolution" philosophy, theology, along with
history, was seen as needing continual and specialized re-
writes.

Harvey Cox in *The Secular City* distilled the ingredients
for a workable revolutionary theory: (1) catalytic, (2)
interpretation of catalepsy, (3) idea of catharsis and (4)
understanding of catastrophe.(29) Moltmann's conception of
hope in its forward moving historical posture fit well into
Cox's scheme. Hope was to become that trained Christian eye
that analyzed the context and served to illumine the catalytic gap. It would draw attention to the difference between
things as they could be, and things as they really were.

Moltmann in *Religion, Revolution and the Future* in 1969
continued to develop his thought. He wrote:

> The new revolutionary situation has brought
> Christianity into a deep *crisis of identity*
> [emphasis mine]. Christians and the
> churches will rediscover their true self-
> consciousness only if they overcome their
> own religious alienation and their own hin-
> drance to the free self-realization of man.(31)

Moltmann observed that the church "narrowly presented the
heavenly Christ in word, sacrament and hierarchy." He saw

revolutionary Christianity as going beyond that and looked
for "communion with the crucified Son of men who waits among
the hungry, the naked, the prisoner, and the refugee for the
acts of righteousness."(32)

Churches that sensed the need to change could be expected
to enter "a deep crisis of identity." Which way should they
turn? In a somewhat similar situation years earlier, Luther
had advocated a return to the Bible, and *sola scriptura*, as
the source of the church's message and as the inspiration
and guide for her practical life.(33) Moltmann offered instead revolutionary change in a process of interacting with
the world. He quoted the comment from Rauschenbusch approv-
ingly: "Ascetic Christianity called the world evil and left
it. Humanity is waiting for a revolutionary Christianity
which will call the world evil and change it."(34)

As theologies evolved, according to Kee's view, the theology of hope evolved into the theology of revolution. Moltmann became a major inspiration for the latter as well. This
development appeared as only a natural implementation of a
hopeful Christianity which saw needs and worked for change.
Revolutionary means were seen as needed, at times, to bring
about change. However, positive results were expected, and
even evidences of love, such as laughter, play and dancing,
were to be looked for in the midst of revolution.

Theology Develops Further

In the late 1960s, the word "revolution" produced adverse
reactions in most Europeans.(35) It was at this time that
a new agenda for European theologians presented itself. It
was the matter of the development of the emerging and newly
articulate Third World countries. The problems of these
countries were being discussed in the secular forum. The
church was invited to join the discussion.

Paul Loffler in a SODEPAX Report from the World Council
of Churches elaborated in 1969 on the acceptable alternative
to revolution, namely a Christian "Theology of Development."

> A mere adaptation of traditional theologi-
> cal positions will not do. . . We need a
> contemporary articulation of faith inter-
> preting theologically the new phenomena, a
> prophetic comment exposing the theological
> content of what is happening to man and by
> men. The other, perhaps less exciting,

> task is to establish connections between
> the issues posed by "development" and the
> main strands of historic Christian think-
> ing. . . . Only *a dialectical interaction*
> [emphasis mine] between the two exercises
> can result in an adequate theological per-
> ception of the processes of development.(36)

To those in the Third World, talk of cooperating in development made them nervous. It sounded as though the inequal-
ity existing between the rich and the poor countries, merely
was to be baptized by western theologians who were too eager
to report their irrelevant views. Okot P'Bitek, in 1970,
spoke to those at the University of Nairobi, "We are not
interested in proving the correctness or validity of this or
that theory of 'progress' or 'development'. . . . "(37)

Yet, to many, there was great attractiveness in the theology of development. It appeared to be truly ecumenical.
It was not originated by any one group. It was a cause for
the drawing together of the Roman Catholic, Orthodox, and
Protestant. Nissiotis described its scope in terms especially
pertinent to the methodology and content of contextualization:

> . . . development concerns the whole man
> and his whole environment, and consequently
> one rightly speaks of *a total effort of
> humanization* [emphasis mine]. . . This
> struggle of humanity towards its full dig-
> nity reveals that man and the world are
> created with a specific purpose, with a
> goal to be attained through a continuous
> process of change and renewal, that goal
> is the reality which has been revealed by
> God in this world in the person of Jesus. . .(38)

"Humanization" became a catchword. It was expected that men
would learn from the mistakes of past history, much as scientists had built on previous research. New and better levels
of society in community were hoped for.

Advocates carefully qualified their hopes. Loffler held
that theology of development did not imply a "perverted"
eschatology which looked for "an imminent historic process
which [would] bring about the Kingdom in this time and world,
etc."(39)   Nikos A. Nissiotis repudiated the charge that the
theology of development was dealing only in "additional or

separate chapters of theology in a post-biblical age." Yet
the theology of development did seem to leave itself open to
criticism that it largely ignored the Bible in preference
for its analytical and speculative theories of development.

To insure biblical influence on secular material Loffler
advocated a dialectical approach:

> In order to isolate the theological issues
> posed by development we cannot follow either
> a merely deductive method, i.e. start from
> given positions in the biblical theology and
> teaching tradition of the Church or follow
> a purely inductive method, i.e. take social,
> economic, and political analysis as the only
> point of departure for theological reflec-
> tion. The assumption is rather that we must
> establish a "dialectical interaction" be-
> tween the issues of development as they are
> posed in the secular discussion and theo-
> logical thinking.(40)

As is readily apparent this dialectical methodology
closely paralleled the theories voiced in the Bossey consultation discussed in Chapter 1. Although other theologies
were to appear on the scene, development theology remained
in force as a major theological position.

A "Liberated" Theology

Along with the impact of development theology, the theology of liberation played a significant role among those who
introduced contextualization of theology. The theology of
liberation had swept across much of the Church in the Third
World by the early 1970s.(41) Mostly formed in the hands of
Third World artisans of theology, mainly in Latin America,
it built on, and in part surpassed, the neo-Marxism and the
secularization theology of Western Europe.(42) Gustavo
Gutierrez described a major aspect of the new theology and
its distinction from development theology in this way:

> In the first place, *liberation* expresses
> the aspirations of oppressed peoples and
> social classes, emphasizing the conflic-
> tual aspect of the economic, social and
> political process. . . In contrast, the
> word *development*, and above all the poli-
> cies characterized as developmentalist

(desarrollista), appear somewhat aseptic,
giving a false picture of a tragic and
conflictual reality.(43)

The charge was not that development was all wrong in its
goal of humanization of man, but supporters of development
had too many vested interests in the existing system. Therefore they could not be expected to advocate radical change.
As a result critics saw development theologians as not at-
tacking "the roots of the evil," failing and causing confusion and frustration.(44) Those in the Third World, who
were coming to realize that they could never win in the old
system whether they played the game right or not, looked for
more radical answers.

Thus, the theology of liberation, much like development
theology, arose in response to a call for it. Miguez-Bonino,
in 1975 after the lines of the theology had become clear,
wrote:

> Commitment, therefore, is born of a ration-
> ality of social analysis and *demands* [empha-
> sis mine] in turn to account for itself in
> theological terms. In this way a new type
> of theological reflection appears integral
> with concrete social and political action.(45)

As Miguez-Bonino saw it, implementation involved working
from two premises, "social analysis" and a "theological" response accounting for the analysis. The methods were ob-
viously related to the approach of the theology of development. It was definitely "a new type of theological reflection" when compared to the mainly deductive approaches of
confessional scholars and the mainly subjective, inductive
approaches of neo-orthodox and liberal thinkers. Yet liberation theology also was clearly related to the political
theologies that had gone before it. The new theology, itself, claimed to draw from much theologizing that had gone
before, Miguez-Bonino noted:

> Protestant Barthian and post-Barthian theol-
> ogy, Roman Catholic conciliar and post-
> conciliar thought, with their common empha-
> sis on the dynamism of God in action, the
> historical character of the Christian faith,
> the concreteness of the incarnation, the
> future oriented nature of an eschatological
> faith--all of this has had a very significant
> influence.(46)

The result was a theology amenable to many in the Third World. To those in Latin America, for example, who were in ecclesiastical positions and familiar with modern theologies, the theological premise was quite familiar. Those less theologically conversant, who rather were more politically active and socialist in belief, were equally at home with the social analysis aspects of the theology of liberation. The goal was for each wing to inform, and integrate with, the other. The result was expected to be Christian concrete social and political action.

Since the advent of higher-criticism of the Bible, those who accepted it had to look elsewhere to find or at least to complete their base for theologizing. By the time the theology of liberation came on the scene, the Bible and those theologies that were formulated in the after-glow of the Bible-based theologies, had been left largely behind. A brief analysis of the very first chapter of Peruvian priest Gustavo Gutierrez' *A Theology of Liberation*, should make this clear. The opening paragraph is especially pertinent to this discussion:

> Theological reflection--that is, the understanding of the faith--*arises spontaneously* [emphasis mine] and inevitably in the believer, in all those who have accepted the gift of the Word of God. Theology is intrinsic to a life of faith seeking to be authentic and complete and is, therefore, essential to the common consideration of this faith in the ecclesial community. There is present *in all believers*--and more so in every Christian community-- *a rough outline of a theology*. There is present an effort to understand the faith, something like a pre-understanding of that faith which is manifested in life, action and concrete attitude. It is on this foundation, and only because of it, that the edifice of theology--in the precise and technical sense of the term--can be erected. This foundation is not merely a jumping off point, but the soil into which theological reflection stubbornly and permanently sinks its roots and from which it derives its strength.(47)

Equivocation of terms could be a problem in interpreting
the above quote. Terms such as "the faith," "the Word of
God," "theology," "concrete attitude" prove to be invested,
upon further discussion in his book, with different meanings
than at first might be supposed. "The faith" turns out to
be the modern system of belief that is derived through
"action-reflection." The contrast of Gutierrez' "the faith"
with "the faith" understood among Evangelicals was
well illustrated in the book *Ministry in Context* which
came out in 1972. (48) It contrasted the evangelical
concept of theology, "an understanding of the Gospel
as propositional truth," with the product of theological
reflection," a free, flexible word which liberates men
and sends them into the midst of the struggle for
justice in the world." (49)

Gutierrez did not go to the Bible as his source or "soil"
for theology. Rather, he posited an instant inner theology
that each *"believer"* has. This intuited "word" was to be
validated in action, and usually in an action done corpor-
ately. He wrote of modern trends which provided "a new form
for seeing the presence and activity of the Church in the
world as a starting point for theological reflection."(50)

It is to be noted that theology was not considered to be
a "deposit of the faith" by liberation theologians but rather
something fluid. Its key characteristic was that it was to
be rooted in, and relevant to a given situation. The concept was more refined than the blunt statement of pragmatism,
"if it works it must be true." Yet truth "in reflection"
was to be validated by the evaluation that it was relevant
and that it *worked*. The thinking of Hegel, Feuerbach and
Marx had done much to inform and influence liberation theologians. Gutierrez explained: ". . . it is to a large extent due to Marxism's influence that theological thought,
searching for its own sources [emphasis mine] has begun to
reflect on the meaning of the transformation of this world
and the action of man in history."(51)

Undoubtedly this influence of Marxism "to a large extent"
is one reason for liberation theology's fondness for action-
reflection. Moltmann's historicizing and historiography
also encouraged the methodology. Especially adopted were
the emphases both on "eschatology and on its implications
on the level of social praxis."(52) More will be said on
praxis below.

Apart from the influence of Marx and Moltmann, several
other sources influenced liberation theology. Roman Catholic

thought, especially since the Medellin Conference in 1968, had been significant. Dogmatic theology came into play, yet, it was a new type of "dogmatics." Karl Rahner wrote "Dogmatic theology today has to be theological anthropology, and. . . such an anthropocentric orientation of theology is both necessary and fruitful."(53) Such a theology of "man's critical reflection on himself,"(54) and "a clear and critical attitude regarding economic and socio-cultural issues" (55) fits well the famous dictum of Protagoras. With human praxis being the measure of all philosophy and theology, both are reduced to anthropology.(56)

Writing in the late 1960s, C. Peter Wagner began to see a clear trend in the movement:

> At times one gets the feeling that the starting point of this group has been an *a priori* socio-economic theory, and that theology has been called in only as an afterthought, not to say rationalization. The Bible seems to be used very often as a source book for proof texts rather than the touchstone of all doctrine.(57)

Wagner seemed to be a bit uncomfortable with his analysis and attempted to soften the blow of his "admittedly harsh criticism" by pointing out that his remarks did not apply equally to all in the "radical left."(58) Yet when one substitutes the word "sundown" for "afterthought," as in the following quote, and when one substitutes the word "premises" (59) for "proof texts", the methodology of the liberation theologians becomes plain. It seems as if the following sentences of Gutierrez were written as a clarification and verification of Wagner's words:

> Theology *follows*; it is the second step. What Hegel used to say about philosophy can likewise be applied to theology; it rises only at sundown. The pastoral activity of the Church does not flow as a conclusion from theological premises. Theology does not produce pastoral activity; rather it reflects upon it.(60)

Praxis, not *theoria*, became the focal point. Praxis became the criteria of truth. According to Dahl, theology was virtually sublated into praxis. The result of that was the "distinct turn from theological concerns to social and economic concerns as being paramount."(61)

The exact meaning of "praxis" in this sense is not to be assumed. It does not simply mean action or practice. It was recently defined by David Tracy as "the critical relationship between theory and practice whereby each is dialectically influenced and transformed by the other."(62)

Again, the concern was for a relevant synthesis that involved a putting-into-action by its very definition. It comes as no surprise, then, considering the corporate and Marxist emphases of the movement, that when political and social issues were considered (in fact they were emphasized) the theories of socialism were stressed.

As politics and anthropology emerged as main issues in liberation theology, church and world seemed to merge somehow into one. Activity was to become earth-centered. Secular tools were to be utilized and the results expected were to be a better world brought about by "the church." "Salvation" took on a different tone, if not a different nature as it was viewed by Gutierrez in a universal sense:

> The unqualified affirmation of the universal will of salvation has radically changed the way of conceiving the mission of the Church in the world. It seems clear today that the purpose of the Church is not to save in the sense of "guaranteeing heaven." The work of salvation is a reality which occurs in history.(63)

Dahl reacted to this paragraph in Gutierrez as follows:

> If the real problem of man, the *radical* problem to use Marx' phrase, is economic and political oppression, and not sin in the heart of the individual; and if salvation is offered to *all* regardless of their awareness of the salvific work, it becomes much easier to understand the *raison d'etre* of Liberation Theology.
>
> Accompanying this soteriological perspective is a dialectical view of history. Thus, the Bible itself must be translated in a new and fresh way for our time—a political hermeneutic that takes into account the axiom of class conflict.(64)

A Theology of "Blackness"

There are many affinities between liberation theology in Latin America and black theology in North America. And as it will be shown below, Moltmann's criticism of Miguez-Bonino, that liberation theology merely has been borrowed from Europe, could apply, in some degree, to black theology as well. Yet black theology is a distinct school of thought.

Much of black theology's uniqueness lies in its roots. Blacks in the United States won emancipation in the 1860's. Yet in practice and in their history, they remained a people cut off from their rights and their heritage. Chancellor Williams surveyed the problem in Africa in his book *The Destruction of Black Civilization: Great Issues of a Race from 4500 B.C. to 2000 A.D.* The process of colonization and the slave trade wrought havoc in Africa. He recorded that

> . . . the really big thing was to change
> the Blacks into Christians, which changed
> them into Westerners, which was to change
> them into the white man's image. . . the
> outcome of which caused Blacks to reject
> and become ashamed of both their culture
> and themselves--the only people on earth
> to do so.(66)

Export of slaves to America only complicated the matter. Although many undoubtedly found salvation and succor in the saving knowledge of Christ, many did not. Many experienced the church as another arm of the oppression forced upon blacks by whites.

In the 1960's black theology, as such, came on the scene. Dr. James H. Cone of Union Theological Seminary, New York, was the leading theologian of the movement. In the form propagated by Cone it was labeled by some as merely another folk religion.(67) Yet, at least one evangelical sought to defend its existence, although not all its premises, by pointing out that it struggled to fill in the gaps left by those who theologized about the "honky Christ" who was only the god of whiteness, middle class morality, and oppression of the black man.(68) More than gaps served to stimulate the writing of a black theology. Supreme Court decisions, rampant hopes and a flexible privatized hermeneutic played a part as well.(69)

Black writers in America agree that the black experience
has been, and is, that the black lacks self-confidence, is
still lynched today, and needs liberation from class oppression. This dehumanized minority sought a fully realized
humanity in a form almost eschatological in nature, and a
creed of liberation was articulated that had room for almost
nothing else. Black theologians came to Scripture with a
definite preoccupation in mind and asked, "Is there anything
here to help me articulate my passion?" The hermeneutics of
"Blackness" that developed tended to make heavy use of motifs and borrowed extensively from the thought of Black
Power, Black Islam, and the civil rights movement.

A Definition

A definition of black theology must begin by making clear
what black theology is not. As mentioned above, it is not
conservative-evangelical theology.(70) Neither is it a
transplanted African theology, although black theology has
been transplanted to South Africa. John S. Mbiti compared
the two as follows:

> . . . one would hope that theology arises
> out of a spontaneous joy in being a Chris-
> tian, responding to life and ideas as one
> redeemed. Black Theology, however, is
> full of sorrow, bitterness, anger and
> hatred. . . asking for what black Americans
> should have had from the start--freedom,
> justice, a fair share in the riches of
> their country, equal opportunities in
> social, economic and political life.(71)

James Cone was one who saw true Christianity manifested
in the Black Power movement. He placed heavy stress on community: the black *community*, liberation of the *community*,
sin as defined by the *community*.(72) Black theology as Cone
wrote it, was an attempt to articulate God's work in the
black world. As he saw it: ". . . black rebellion is a
manifestation of God himself actively involved in the
present-day affairs of men and for the purpose of liberating
a [emphasis mine] people."(73)

A source perhaps more representative than Cone, the National Committee of Black Churchmen, surveyed oppression
around them and considered their work redemptive for the
future. Defining black theology, they wrote:

> It seeks to plumb the black condition in
> the light of God's revelation by Jesus
> Christ, so that the black community can
> *see that the gospel is commensurate with*
> *the achievement of black humanity* [empha-
> sis mine]. . . This is the message of
> Black Theology. In the words of Eldridge
> Cleaver, "We shall have our manhood. We
> shall have it or the earth will be leveled
> by our efforts to gain it."(74)

Liberal and neo-orthodox theologies were relied on for
inspiration. Higher critical views set the standards for
biblical criticism. Mbiti described the methodology as
drawing from "Black experience" and "in a more general way
from the Scriptures. . . ."(75)

Sin

Sin is seen in the Bible in two aspects, sin as guilt,(76)
and sin as power.(77) Guilt has to do with sins committed.
Christ has redeemed us from this guilt if we are "in" him.
Sin as power relates to the present and sin working in us
and against the desires of our new nature. Cone seemed to
categorize it differently: Individual and corporate sins
were considered to have been dealt with. The only sin of
significance in terms of the present were those that affected
the life of the community.

Spiritual sin was relegated to the past where Christ the
victor despoiled Satan and broke his tyranny. The sinful
"evil forces" there lost their power to force us into slavery.(78) In Barthian style Cone proposed that *all* could
know that they were free. The crucial battle had been won
already on the cross. That being dispensed with, the only
sins left to be of concern would be those evil forces which
enslave contemporary man. To Cone, when one lived in black
America, those forces were legion.

Perhaps to Cone, the most momentous sin of all was the
oppression of blacks. Cone wrote, "Sin. . . for black people is the loss of [black identity].(79) He suggested that
the true nature of sin was perceived "only in the moment of
oppression and liberation," that men come to "know what non-
being [sin] is because they have experienced being [Black
Power]."(80) Using a rather circular approach, he linked
knowledge of sin with immediate history:

> Since sin is inseparable from revelation,
> and since revelation is an event that
> takes place in the moment of liberation
> from oppression, there can be no knowl-
> edge of the sinful condition except in
> the movement of an oppressed community
> claiming its freedom.(81)

Keeping in mind Barth's emphasis that sin and its power
is only a convincing will-o-the-wisp that oppresses us, it
was to be expected that Cone sought to break the spell cast
on the black community. As men were to be "educated out"
of the miasma, hope would rise that they were to be truly
liberated from *human* oppression as well. Thus Jesus' work
became "essentially one of liberation. Becoming a slave
himself, he opens realities of human existence formerly
closed to man."(82)

The problem had been compounded because the American society as a whole was seen as blind to the true nature of
sin. Black society, however, could see it because it had
experienced oppression. Great solidarity was felt between
the oppressed Israelite community in Egypt and the modern
black community. To be "in sin" was seen as meaning "to
deny the community."(83) The community that was being de-
nied was the black community. Whites were doing the oppres-
sing. Therefore to be saved meant (1) to be involved in
the community as a black or at least as a black "in spirit,"
and (2) to be actively involved in strengthening the black
community.(84)

Humanization of blacks seemed to be Cone's ultimate goal
for Christianity. This humanization was to be enjoyed more
and more by the fuller community. Cone suggested that
"salvation is by the free grace of God."(85) Yet following
his logic to its end, he stated that such a saved man would
become "a rebel against humanity and injustice."(86) Saved
man affirmed that freedom which was his. He was then to act
as a full man. To fail to do so was to act as the Narnian
trolls who though seated on the Elysian fields thought themselves to be caged in the gloom of a dirty prison stall.

Cone's work has several serious problems. Those who
would follow his method must first see if removing these
objections leaves anything significant of the theology which
he has formulated. Jones and Mbiti rightly saw that Cone
tends towards espousal of a folk religion. One would expect
a full spectrum of theological comment. Yet the theme

black liberation from societal oppression is basically
the only message.(87)

Another significant difficulty is that Cone seemed to
adopt wholeheartedly the ideological work of the Black Power
movement, assuming its purity, apparently, because of the
expected cauterizing experience of oppression. From this
position he then had to try to inject Christian values into
the ideologically closed system. The hoped-for end seemed
to be a "Christianized" Black Power movement.(88) However,
one must have serious reservations about assuming that the
goals of the Black Power movement, or any other movement,
are identical with the goals of Christ for his church.

Political Theologies and the Consultation of 1971

The basic parallels between the 1971 consultation on dogmatic or contextual theology(89) and the political theologies should be evident. (1) *Higher criticism*, which cannot
be refuted in the scope of this text yet must be considered
too radical in its mistreatment of the Bible, had given to
those who accepted it, a Bible which could not give an authoritative content to theology. (2) *Systematic Theology*
was seen as being rooted in contexts largely irrelevant to
most, if not all, present contexts. Thus, the cultural an-
tiques contained in systematic or dogmatic theology were rejected. Alas, much of the theologizing done in the past
which was solidly based on the Bible, was also jettisoned.
(3) The way of evaluating *history*, exemplified in Moltmann,
was part of this interaction with systematic theology.
Looking to a future point of *promise*, from which history was
to be evaluated, he removed from history and the present
most heretofore accepted truth statements. What remained
were a few motifs; "promise", "hope", "action", "open opportunities", and the like.

An end result of 1, 2, and 3 above, was that much that
normally gives meaning to life and theology was evacuated
of content. The content then had to come, necessarily, from
other sources. The heavy reliance on Hegel, Feuerbach, Marx,
Bloch, and the social sciences has been documented. An almost desperate emphasis was placed on relevance. This
seemed to be much of the motivation behind these works. The
relative value of culture and its benign nature was tacitly
assumed. Fragments of insight and concentration were developed in various cultures. These fragments of theology,
such as a theology of road building in Chicago, were then
joined into a larger theological mosaic. A philosophical-

theological-ideological framework was to be utilized in order to avoid development of a theology that was merely a
pile of fragments--insights that changed to the color of the
context much as a chameleon changes color in response to
changes in its environment. Some insights were joined geo-
graphically--African; some racially--black; some philosophi-
cally--development, liberation. The fragments were to interact dialectically within the philosophical framework and
also in relation to theological motifs or insights of past-
oriented theologies.

3

Contextualization:
The Public Pronouncement

In 1972 the two years set aside for the study committee of
the TEF, which encompassed discussions and developments such
as the Bossey consultation considered in Chapter I, came to
an end. The committee's task during that decisive period
was "to discern more clearly the new issues and the new
challenges in theological education seen in the context of
the radical changes on the world scene, particularly in the
Third World."(1) The two years were spent in intensive study.
The TEF staff, and members of the study committee, worked in
collaboration with theological associations and other people
and institutions engaged in theological education. Discerned
by the researchers was the need to implement theological education "with a more flexible way of responding to the living context of our situation in the world of today."(2)

TEF was encouraged in its task. It was hoped that substantial results might come of its labors because it aimed
at leadership training. The chairman of the committee suggested that "the secret of the renewal of the church is the
renewal of the clergy."(3) Such "renewal" was seen as a
distinct change in direction. Changes in thought as well as
in structures were to be fostered.

The problems of the Third World were seen by the committee
of the TEF(4) as having a remarkably similar profile to
those of the West.(5) This likeness was attributed to traditional western patterns of residential institutions inherited
by the Third World. Interaction between the Third World and
the First World was envisioned during the third mandate

period. It was assumed that if problems were the same, answers discovered in the Third World might be useful in the
West, and vice versa. Both areas were seen as having institutions attempting to minister "amid the struggle for liberation and meaning in the chaotic seventies." Both were considered one "in our common search for renewed authenticity
in theological education."(6) If the task could be accom-
plished the results were expected to be far-reaching.

Results of the second mandate had been significant. About
352 individual grants were made for higher degrees of research. The major emphasis was in Africa "where the ratio
between nationals and expatriates rose to one to one in contrast to [the] former ratio of one to four."(7) But as
these grants were being given out, and other second mandate
assignments were being followed up, the world grew notice-
ably turbulent. The disruptive forces and rapid social
changes that drew the attention of the political theologians
were also concerning the TEF. According to the background
material in *Ministry in Context*, the direction of the third
mandate developed as "the traditional life patterns and ways
of thinking both in the church and the world, were called
into question." In conscious response to these pressures
"there was radical rethinking of mission, ministry and theology, which affected the whole of theological education."'
The result was a "very strong call for return and renewal
in theological education."(8) The changes were to be both
in the form, and in the content, of theological education.
A description of the pressures that demanded response is
reproduced below:

> The determinant goal is that the Gospel
> be expressed, and ministry undertaken,
> *in response to*:
> a) The widespread crisis of faith and
>   search for meaning in life;
> b) The urgent issues of human develop-
>   ment and social justice; and
> c) The dialectic between a universal
>   technological civilization and local
>   culture and religious situations.(9)

It must be noted that a, b, and c above all have their
antecedents in both the Consultation and the theology discussed in the previous two chapters. Issues of human *development* and social justice were encountered in the discussion
on the political theologies of development and liberation.
The widespread crisis of faith was a key problem in the

European church, as a whole, against which the political
theologians were reacting. And a dialectical method was
strongly advocated by almost all those involved. More precisely, the TEF's considered response to the changing world
was to:

   a) encourage relevant and indigenous
      theological reflection and expres-
      sion, including that which arises
      out of dialogue among the living
      faiths of man;
   b) examine and experiment with theo-
      logical curriculum and teaching
      methodology, and
   c) analyze and experiment with semi-
      nary structure, support and adminis-
      tration. (10)

To consider these suggestions of the third mandate which
came out in 1970, the study committee held its first meeting
in Kampala, Uganda, in July 1971, approximately simultaneous
with the Consultation in Bossey. At the second meeting in
Bromley, July 1972, the "working policy" was produced. The
policy's main concern was "emphasis on contextuality and
contextualization as the way towards renewal and reform in
theological education."(11) The TEF was serious about reform,
and contextualization was seen as *the* answer. They said,
"It may be stated that contextualization should be the focal
concern because *through it alone* [emphasis mine] will come
reform and renewal. Contextualization of the Gospel is a
missiological necessity."(12) It may be observed also that
the main thrust was *theological* reform.

The major portion of the "working policy" was formulated
by the staff and was derived largely from the issue papers
produced by them. Therefore both the discussion summary and
the issue papers will be considered in this section to determine more precisely what the TEF in 1972 considered contextualization to be.(13)

Discussing the two-year study period, the staff members
revealed some of their presuppositions and conclusions:

      In all this process we have seen that theo-
      logical education is once again in travail,
      and that everywhere basic questions are be-
      ing raised. It is important that we should
      be *open* [emphasis mine] to *the signs of the*

> *time* and especially to the leading of the
> Holy Spirit, believing that the current
> missiological challenges are at the root
> of the *radical rethinking* of ministry, *of
> theology*, and consequently of theological
> education as a whole.
>
> We have come to the end of an era. . .(14)

This "radical rethinking" was to be "fragmentary and provisional" and was to take the form of "theological reflection."(15) This concept, reflection, could be considered
crucial in the TEF's methodology for reform. "Theological
reflection" as a method permeated the thought of the group.
Reflection seemed to be in contradistinction to exegesis.
It was very close to, if not identical with, the praxis emphasis in political theology. TEF expressed its method as
"theologia viatorum," a term used by Jurgen Moltmann.

Behind the emphasis on theological reflection may be discerned the belief in revelation as encounter, a tenet of
neo-orthodoxy. This includes a basic objection to propositional truth, and the belief that *no* revelation can communicate cognitive information. Ronald Nash summed up the position as follows:

> The disjunction between personal and pro-
> positional revelation is exclusive because
> cognitive knowledge about God is unattain-
> able. Because God is totally transcendent,
> because he is unlike anything else in our
> experience, human language is an unfit in-
> strument to capture ideas or express truths
> about God. Nor are man's rational facul-
> ties adequate to allow him to have knowl-
> edge about the transcendent. Cognitive
> knowledge of God is unattainable. . . rev-
> elation must be by personal encounter;
> there is no alternative.(16)

Reflecting this position the TEF sought to discern God in
historical, contextually limited encounters.

Emphasis on "theological reflection" reveals another
theme of the TEF. Contextualized theology was to be a *pro-
gressive* theology. The "genuine encounter between God's
Word and His World" was to lead to revelation understood in
a new way. And that new way, itself, might be superseded in
the future.

As the "working policy" itself is considered below, this infeeding of the terminology, content, and methodologies of political theology, and more obliquely, neo-orthodoxy, must be kept constantly in mind.

The "Working Policy" Considered(17)

The working policy authorized the TEF to seek $3,300,000 during the third mandate period.(18) The working definition of contextualization was formulated as "the capacity to respond meaningfully to the Gospel within the framework of one's own situation." (19)

It may be asked whether or not many in conciliar circles and in evangelical circles have been misled by this passage (below) which seems at first glance to define contextualization as merely a form of updated indigenization, requiring only better methods of communication and the like.

> It [contextualization] means all that is implied in the familiar term "indigenization" and yet seeks to press beyond. Contextualization has to do with how we assess the peculiarity of third world contexts. Indigenization tends to be used in the sense of responding to the Gospel in terms of a traditional culture. Contextualization, while not ignoring this, takes into account the process of secularity, technology, and the struggle for human justice, which characterize the historical moment of nations in the Third World.(20)

Byang Kato, at the International Congress on World Evangelization, held at Lausanne, Switzerland, in 1974, thought this passage referred to communication.(21) So have many evangelicals involved in missions work. As Knapp has written: "The danger for conservative evangelicals (especially missiologists) is to view contextualization as warmed-over indigenization. The TEF documents are careful to ward off this misunderstanding."(22) Whether the TEF equivocated or was careful in definition is irrelevant at this point. Most evangelicals have *not* understood what TEF was saying. The double-premise of theology and the dialectical method employed have not been discerned. Instead of looking for relevance *within* theology as TEF has structured a theology hoped to be contextually relevant, evangelicals have assumed a

common gospel and have encouraged "contextualization," what-
ever that has meant to them,(23) and given strong warnings
against syncretism, those accretions of theological error
that cling when theology is communicated through a culture's
conceptual screen.(24)

It must be realized that if both groups speak of "contextualization" and intend to move beyond "indigenization," they
both move beyond in different directions. The TEF changes
theology, methodologically attaching its theological formulating to context and framework. Evangelicals pay closer
attention to culture and method but do not change much of
their theology, a policy which has inherent strengths and
weaknesses.(25)

In the policy in *Ministry in Context*, the assumed close
relationship between the First and Third Worlds was clearly
evidenced, and largely justified, within limits. Those in
the Third World countries probably tended to see fewer parallels than TEF suggested. The theologians of liberation,
for example, claimed uniqueness but drew heavily from the
Europeans Marx and Moltmann. Those in the West assumed,
perhaps, more parallels than actually existed. The Third
World's sharp reaction to development theology serves to
underline this point.(26) Working from the mandate of 1970,
and assuming the connection of the two worlds which no doubt
allowed the problems and tentative answers of the West to be
imposed to some extent on the Third World, the policy discerned four areas to be contextualized. These were (1)
missiology, (2) theological approach, (3) educational
method and (4) educational structure. (At this point the
reader is encouraged to read the central portion of the
working policy which is reproduced in Appendix B.)

The working policy is best understood from several perspectives. The first is that of background. This has been
presented in chapters one and two. This background helps
one to understand why the policy speaks of "radical changes,"
or being "hopeful for what is yet to come," of "a message of
liberation," of "theological reflection," and of "the particular situation."(27)

The second perspective is to look at the four major areas
to be contextualized. It must not be forgotten that these
four areas and all contexts were considered to be interde-
pendent. The policy stated: "Contextualization. . . means
that the possibilities for renewal must first of all be
sensed locally and situationally, yet always within the

framework of contemporary interdependence which binds both
to the problems of the past and present to the possibilities
for the future."(28) Of course, this "interdependence" relates to the concept of framework. Such a framework would
be above any local context and would inform the evaluation
of, or the relating of, or perhaps even the formulating of
the actual contextualizing.

Of the four areas pinpointed by TEF the most crucial to
this discussion was "contextualization in theological approach."(29) A dialectical methodology in doing theology,
as shown above, was liable to produce a radical change in
theology as traditionally formulated. Thus "theological
approach" was to be significant in terms of theological *content*. (30) This theological approach and content would then
be closely tied in with methodology, pedagogy and structure.
(31) TEF's belief in the relationship of theology to pedagogy and structure was revealed in the policy's section on
extension theological education. TEE (or theological education by extension as it has been commonly termed by evangelicals) is definitely an alternate form of education from the
traditional residence or correspondence schools. Yet as a
definite alternative structure for education it was considered suspect because of its theological ties. The policy
asked:

> . . . is it because the method itself has
> a hidden agenda, a conservative ideology
> and pedagogy more at home with an under-
> standing of the Gospel as propositional
> truth than as a free, flexible Word which
> liberates men and sends them into the
> midst of the struggle for justice in the
> world?(32)

The point here is that TEF believed in close ties between
theology and pedagogy and structure. The question needs to
be asked: Is the methodology of contextualizing theology
as closely or even more closely tied to political theology
as it was feared that TEF was tied to evangelical theology?
Is it possible, if one does not hold to "a free, flexible
Word" but rather to propositional truth, to contextualize
conservative evangelical theology? Defenders of propositional truth must not blithely assume that they are remain-
ing true to their heritage and professed beliefs if they
readily incorporate transitory elements into their epistemological base.(33)

Kosuke Koyama saw a strong theme in the working policy of TEF: "TEF theological reflection locates the ultimate moment of such authentic contextualization in the incarnation of Jesus Christ."(34)   Indeed, the TEF saw contextualization as "a theological necessity demanded by the incarnational nature of the Word."(35)   It can also be added that *incarnational* evangelism was envisioned in the implementation of the *Missio Dei*.

On the matter of TEF's stress on incarnational thinking, Stephen Knapp believes that what was referred to

> seems to involve the transition from church to the world as the central focus of God's redeeming activity, with a broadening out of this activity from the traditional pre-occupation, with personal salvation towards the accomplishment of reconciliation, humanization, and more recently, liberation, in the general historical process.(36)

Thus the church was to become a servant to those processes affecting reconciliation and humanization on behalf of or even along with the living Christ working in general history.(37)

When one combines this view with the thought that just as Christ represented God in the world after his incarnation, so Christians incarnate God in today's world, a radical change from evangelical missiology and theology is effected. Knapp evaluates it as follows: ". . . the transition is not merely from a static to a dynamic and from a past-oriented to a present-oriented construction. It is from a church-oriented to a world-oriented one as well."(38)

This change in emphasis might be misunderstood. When, however, one is familiar with the TEF's call for radical change and reform, compares the parallels in contextualism with, and notes the *universalism* in, the political theologies, then it seems all of a piece.

In seeking to go beyond indigenization, the TEF saw an important new element in modern cultures world-wide. Technology had impinged on all society. As has been noted, isolated tribes had become familiar with the sound of a transistor radio. One man from the Third World evaluated his own culture and found that he moved within eleven different cultural contexts. Modern life had become complex and was

continually changing. Contextualism as presented by the TEF
sought to relate not only to the indigenous or traditional
culture but also sought to take into account "the process of
secularity, technology, and the struggle for human justice."
(39) These attempts at focused attention also recognized
the "continually changing nature of every human situation."
(40) In a curiously worded, but clear statement, the TEF
almost personified relevance. *"Relevance* [emphasis mine]
takes contextuality seriously by discerning God's mission
for man in history; *it* must also do so *intelligently*, understanding the contextual issues and their signficance."(41)
These thoughts were applied to the *Missio Dei*. They are
seen as directly relating to the mission of the church.
Relevance was to be part of the framework that picks and
chooses what contextual fragments are worthy of attention.
Such comments seem to beg the question: relevant to whom?
Rather than asserting that relevance determines which contextual elements of theology will be considered strategic and
presumably will be emphasized, it might have been expected
that more might have been said, and necessarily must be said,
as to the criteria for such a choice. The most natural criteria for the TEF seem to have been those contextual fragments, themes and motifs considered strategic by political
theologies.

The TEF had to decide what methodology to use to stay
relevant to the changing world. The TEF chose to keep theology current in history by making the current of history
part of theology! A dialectic was envisioned. Such a tech-
nique was not new, as such. But the results were, and were
considered by some as revelation. This was due in part to
the lack of distinction made between special and general
revelation. The dialectic operated in this way: "Authentic
contextualization is. . . arising always out of a genuine
encounter between (1) God's Word and (2) His world. . . ."
The result or synthesis of this encounter was always to be
placed in a framework.

The Study Papers

Eight areas of concern were determined by the TEF. These
areas were the categories under which one could apply for
financial assistance.(42) They were: (1) "advanced study
centres," (2) "research projects and grants for students of
renewing significance within existing institutions for theological training." This area included curriculum revisions
and programs emphasizing "practical training and ministerial
reformation."

(3) "Extension Theological Education [TEE]." This included projects aimed at cooperation between "the conservative evangelical churches and those more ecumenically oriented. . . for more authentically contextual forms of theological training." The majority of TEE programs being of
the former group, this meant *changing* or "improving. . .
methodology and content of extension theological education."
The leadership in conservative evangelical TEE circles was
targeted by the TEF study paper prepared for this section.
People such as Bruce Nicholls were specifically referred to.
In a later section this comment was made: "(b) Encourage
the developers of extension programs [emphasis mine] to re-
tain the strengths of a *historical-critical* [!] way of doing
theology. . . ." (43)

In addition, evangelicals were to add the TEE "fire" while
ecumenicals were expected to add "the flavor."

> (e) Wherever possible, help bridge what in
> some places is a growing gap between the
> conservative evangelical and the ecumeni-
> cal churches, on the assumption that *the*
> *evangelical commitment of the former is a*
> *needed lever for the social concerns of*
> *the later and visa versa* [emphasis mine].(44)

(4) "Forms of theological education alternative *[sic?]* to
the traditional residential pattern." These programs were
specifically encouraged to "do theology 'in via' or 'in involvement,' on the one hand, and to implement methodological
issues such as the interaction between action and reflection
on the other . . . ." The theological affinities of such
propositions should be clear. Also advocated was a dialectical approach: "the tension between quality in thought and
action."(45) (5) "Faculty development." (6) Associations."
These associations were to be encouraged to have more involvement in the *theology* of their member institutions. Such
theology was to be of the contextual type.

(7) "Teaching methodology and theological curriculum."
This area emphasized orientation toward "liberation and missions" and an "understanding of education as a dialogical
process between the Gospel and the particular socio-cultural
situation." Theological stress was to be consistent with
the entire project: ". . . vivid teaching demands more, not
less, in the way of disciplined theological reflection."
(8) "Educational media." These were to include textbooks,
library grants, subsidy to theological journals, ad hoc

publications and other communications media. All were to be
considered in light of TEF's four-fold principle of contextuality.

    Among the staff papers is one on "The Central Issue:
Contextualization." Two brief paragraphs from it are reproduced below.

> 1) Missiological contextualization. Is
> the school, centre or undertaking seeking
> to develop a style of training which fo-
> cuses upon the urgent issues of renewal
> and reform in the churches, and upon the
> vital issues of human development and
> justice in its particular situation?. . .
>
> 2) Theological contextualization. Is
> the school, centre or undertaking seeking
> to do theology in a way appropriate and
> authentic to its situation? Does it of-
> fer an approach and theological training
> which seeks to relate the Gospel more
> directly to urgent issues of ministry and
> service in the world? Does it move out
> of its own cultural milieu in its expres-
> sion of the Gospel?(46)

    A final observation to be made in *Ministry in Context* is
the noticeable overlap in personnel, with those considered
in chapters one and two. Only one will be mentioned, as an
example.

    Paul Loffler, who was presented by Alistair Kee as a theo-
logian of development, was a resource person for the TEF.
TEF quotes him in the staff paper on "Some Types of Alternative Forms." The double-premise dialectic of contextualization and development theology is quite evident: "The methodology implicit is that of 'theology as process;' which con-
sists in 'interaction between *involvement and reflection*'
and 'interaction between the *response of the people of God
today* to the Mission of God today and the *records of past
response and action.*'"[emphasis mine](47) TEF's comment
on the above quote was not to its appropriateness or to question its obvious predilections. Rather it was to question
whether or not such an approach was not only applicable to
the area where Loffler applied it, but to other areas.

Loffler's methodology was presented more clearly in his article of 1969, "The Sources of a Christian Theology of Development."(48) "The assumption is. . . that we must establish a 'dialectical interaction' between the issues of development as they are posed in the secular discussion and theological thinking."(49)

With the public introduction of the term contextualization by TEF, many have sought to contextualize. Some merely appropriated the term to cover their own activities already in progress.(50) Those who operated in accord with TEF assumptions,(51) described above, might be labeled as "technical contextualization." (52)

Theology in the Americas

One of the most clear-cut ideological proponents of technical contextualization is the movement known as Theology in the Americas. This movement, related to the National Council of churches of Christ in the USA, held a theological conference in Detroit in August of 1975.

Preparation for the conference covered about a year. For some months prior to the conference about sixty "reflection groups" around the United States met to prepare for it. To a limited degree the conference format and program included the combined reflection and analysis of many different groups.

Two documents provided by the Secretariat of Theology in the Americas will be the main sources for the following comments (see Appendices C and D for the reproductions of these documents).(53) The parallels between TEF and Theology in the Americas will be obvious to the reader and will be pointed out only incidentally until the conclusion of this section when they will be summarized.

Definitions of theology were liberally sprinkled throughout the documents. It was first of all agreed that theology as understood by this group meant "a difference in the understanding of theology."(54) There was also agreement that "theology is the acceptance of the Divine Revelation in Jesus Christ."(55) One might presume that the "difference" in theology came from a difference in defining "the Divine Revelation." And this would seem to be the case. Some theologians were quoted as defining theology as "critical reflection on the historical praxis."(56) Praxis was defined as "practice associated with a total dynamics of

historical vision and social transformation. . . Since praxis
changes the world as well as the actors it becomes the
starting point for a clearer vision of God in history."(57)

Coupled with the changed definitions came a "new way of
knowing."(58) As the documents explained it:

> There has been a change in the understand-
> ing of truth, in the sociology of knowledge
> in general and in *theology* [emphasis mine]
> in particular. Thinking is not now con-
> sidered prior or superior to action, rather,
> it takes place in action. The Christian
> religion was founded not on a word, but on
> the Word made Flesh. Faith is no longer
> simply "applied" or "completed" in action,
> but for its very understanding (and this
> is *theology*) faith *demands* that it be dis-
> covered in action.(59)

The passage in Luke 4:18-19 was referred to frequently in
apparent justification for a political emphasis on liberation. This liberation was expected to occur in several areas.
"Liberation is God's intention: liberation from spiritual,
structural and ideological forms of oppression."(60)

Political and/or structural liberation attracted the
heaviest attention. One of the aims of Theology in the Americas was given as "a New Order." Formation of that new order meant "working for new societal structures."(61) This
political thrust was seen as an integral part of being a
Christian in today's world. "Can a Christian today still
confess commitment to Jesus and not be involved politically?"
(62) The answer was quite explicit: "Until political power
is used for human liberation—until the power of the USA
serves the cause of the poor within its own borders and the
poor countries in the world, there can be no rest for American Christians."(63)

The works of Durkeim, Max Weber and Marx were considered
as resource materials for the analysis of the U.S. context.
(64) This input was to interact dialectically with theology
to result in "the appropriation of socio-political analysis
to theology and faith. . ."(65)

A dialectical approach permeated all formulations. In
looking toward a global vision, and the place of contextualized American theology in such a vision, the dialectic was

utilized. "Praxis means action combined with theory; *action shapes theory* [emphasis mine] which then redirects action, and so on--all situated within a global perspective."(66)

The objectives of the "process" for Theology in the Americas reflected the dialectic: ". . . explore new methodologies in dealing with the relationship between: a) truth and practice b) faith and praxis c) ideology and faith."(67)

In its statement on "the epistemology of a reflection which starts from praxis," the documents suggested not two, but what appears to be a theological base of three, or even four, premises:

> This new epistemology (way of knowing) has to be applied to the "revealed truth of Christianity." The theological truth is not only the conformity of the mind to revelation as it is contained Scripture; it is also the discernment of present evil in the world and in hearts, judged by the message of the gospel and the discovery of the movement of redemptive and liberating history. Divine truth is redemptive, but the norm of theclogical truth comes from its role in the ongoing process of world-building.(68)

The synthesis of the various sources was to be used in "shaping a theology for the future."(69) It also appeared that some sort of framework would be involved, aiding in uniting the various contextualized theological insights into a coherent vision: "What is needed is an analysis that will help them to see the connection between local issues and global realities, between national problems and international structures."(70)

Exegesis was seen as a highly suspect methodology for doing theology. Praxis was considered as the only way to know truth in context.(71) In fact, exegetically derived doctrines were seen as irrelevant at best, and even divisive.

> Theology in the Americas believes that the old ecclesiastical and doctrinal disputes that have divided the Church for so long are *not relevant anymore* [emphasis mine]. There is a change in the focus of theology and a change in the methodology of theology.

In the past, the questions in traditional
theology were raised from within the ecclesiastical institutions. Today, while not
abandoning that perspective, Christians and
theologians want to understand the meaning
of the Word of God present as judgment and
grace in history, both personal and social--
of this generation.(72)

Eight projects were developed, aimed at a more specific
implementation of their aims. They were: (1) task force of
professional theologians, (2) women's project, (3) black
theology project, (4) Hispanic consultation, (5) labor and
church dialogue, (6) white theology project, (7) Asian Americans in the U.S. context, (8) land, native Americans and red
theology.

It must be pointed out that Theology in the Americas as
a program intended to do theology itself. Its stress was on
group-thinking, and then on putting theory into practice.
Theory was then to be remade in the doing process. The
Christian experience in community was to play a significant
role in determining theology.

Many aspects of the American context were targeted for
the greatest emphasis, especially societal structures and
economic and political systems. Proponents of socialism
were to be referred to for theoretical framework. Emphasis
was not restricted to the Americas, specifically North America, but concern was paid to the whole world.

Another program, similar and "intrinsically related to
Theology in the Americas,"(73) drew concern. It was Ecumenical Dialogue of Third World Theologians. It was described
as a facilitator of "an ongoing exchange between theologians,
church leaders, and grassroots Christians of Africa, Asia,
and Latin America who attempt to deepen their understanding
of what God's will is for their people today."(74) Its goal
resembled Theology in the Americas and was "to contextualize
theologically the struggle for liberation of Third World
peoples."(75)

"Popular Contextualizers"

Many who jumped on the contextualization bandwagon, after
TEF's introduction of the term in 1972, were not contextualizers in the technical sense. While often using and quoting
the TEF documents, these contextualizers sometimes took

issue with various TEF recommendations. At times the basic underlying framework and principles of technical contextualization did not seem to be clearly perceived. Lacking was the dedicated usage of the dialectic resulting in making context part of the theological context. Political theology, in its more radical forms, was often considered suspect.

In fact, theologically, these people are best placed on a continuum between the radical theologians and evangelicals. Their theology has proven to be in some sense neo-orthodox or liberal. Thus they have been more concerned with use of Scripture than the technical contextualizers. Usually their hermeneutic has been based on the findings of higher criticism.

Something more than *sola scriptura* serves as their authoritative source for theology, as these contextualizers work. This can be traced to their theology, and their hermeneutical methods. As a result, this seems to allow the context, or insights based on their interpretaion of the context, to supplement the teachings of the Bible. This often results in a distorting or negating of the sense of basic biblical doctrines. These contextualizers, whose methodology is distinct both from technical contextualizers and evangelicals, will herein be called "popular contextualizers."(76)

Because technical contextualizers often use biblical terminology and often stress themes labeled as biblical, they can be hard to distinguish from evangelical context-indigenizers. Popular contextualizers add even more confusion to the matter. They frequently refer to the Bible, and often conduct extensive studies of Scripture passages.

A survey of the methodology of the various groups--the technical contextualizers, popular contextualizers, and the evangelical indigenizers--reveals a rough continuum which also reflects the use these groups make of the Bible.(77) Evangelicals who context-indigenize(78) and those who practice indigenization principles, more rigidly defined (These two groups will be considered below; the evangelicals in Chapter IV, and the indigenizers only obliquely in the same chapter) adhere to the Bible as the sole authoritative source for theological content. The contextualizers on the other hand supplement this and distort the biblical teachings more and more as one moves to the left side of the continuum. (See figure 3).

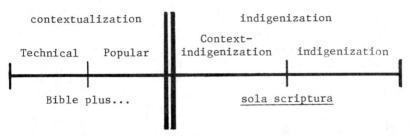

Figure 3: the continuum of those who deal with Christianity and culture. The further one goes from right to left, specifically from the break in the middle of the graph the more one supplements the Bible with other thoughts.

Of those popular contextualizers who seem to distill theology from the context as well as the Bible, two will now be discussed. While exemplifying this type of approach they do not exhaust the category.(79) These two representatives are the Japanese theologian Kosuke Koyama, and the former Professor of New Testament at the Protestant Theological Faculty at Yaounde, Cameroun,(80) Daniel Von Allmen.

Kosuke Koyama, in his book, *Waterbuffalo Theology*,(81) opened his discussion on contextualization by stating his intent to develop a Third World theology. The first task he saw was "raising issues" in distinction to digesting the works of theologians such as Augustine, Barth and Rahner. (82) He did admit, however, his dependence on such writers when trying to decide what theological issues to raise.(83)

Quoting from the major definition passage in *Ministry in Context,*(84) he presented his interpretation of the passage:

> . . . contextualization of theology is
> something more than taking the histori-
> cal and cultural context seriously; it
> is letting theology speak in and through
> that context. This much is already a
> tall order indeed. The TEF concept of
> contextualization "seeks to press beyond"
> this. Theology must consist of critical
> accommodation. This is *authentic contex-*
> *tualization.* TEF theological reflection
> locates the ultimate moment of such au-
> thentic contextualization in the incarna-
> tion of Jesus Christ.(85)

An active posture was to be taken by theologians as they
incarnated the crucified Christ. In this, Koyama agreed
with the theology of the technical contextualizers.(86) In
contrast to the TEF, Koyama appeared to feel quite free in
interchanging the terms "contextualiation" and "indigenization." He also placed a much heavier stress on grassroots
theologizing. In the quote below, he revealed his dislike
of modifying existing theologies:

> Chinese theology cannot come out instantly
> when theology is recast in the Confucion
> category from a neo-Platonic category. If
> that were all it took to contextualize theo-
> logy, it would not be such a difficult ar-
> rangement. It is, in reality, to do with
> the emergence of theological work engaged
> in by a Chinese crucified mind.(87)

Although treating contextualization as such in his chapter one, and applauding the approach, Koyama completed his
Waterbuffalo Theology with a series of insights into the
Buddhist mindset beset by an imposing modern culture. He
discussed these insights without being specific as to the
results of such an approach, and looked for ways to better
communicate his rather ill-defined(88) gospel. He dealt
quite comfortably with several brilliant insights, but did
not force them into political or Marxist frameworks as he
built his popularly contextualized theology.(89)

It has been suggested that Asia is such a large and diverse continent that any work covering many areas must of
necessity be disconnected. An overall integrating framework
which might "connect" Asia is not readily discernible in
his text.(90) His lack of any systematizing or relating-in-
framework, combined with his non-evangelical theology,(91)
sets Koyama off as a popular contextualizer.

Daniel Von Allmen in 1975 published an article in the
International Review of Mission entitled, "The Birth of
Theology: Contextualization as the dynamic element in the
formation of New Testament Theology."(92) In it he described
contextualization as "an attempt to express the fact that the
situation of theology in a process of self-adaptation to a
new or changing context is the same in Europe as in Asia or
in Africa." Such a concept was suspect to Von Allmen, for
it implied to him a "short cut" of "simply adapting an existing theology to contemporary or local task." "Contextualization was also considered, at least in his use of the term,
as a synonym for indigenization.

In dealing with the concept of contextualization, Von Allmen quoted Marc Spindler's observation:

> When Western theologians have given voice to their expectation of an Africanizing or indigenizing of theology, they have met with very marked reserve on the part of indigenous theologians. Their expectation is considered to be both an incitement to heresy and an insufferable sign of paternalism.

Following Spindler's lead, Von Allmen suggested three impasses in the way of those attempting to properly "do theology." The first was paternalism. Into this impasse the African theologian John S. Mbiti was supposed to have blundered. (93) Heresy was a second impasse. (94) And "'contextualization' as an adaptation of an existing theology" was considered as a third impasse. (95)

Von Allmen, in following what he saw as the New Testament pattern, advocated principles appropriate to indigenization:

> No true "indigenization or contextualization" can take place because foreigners, the "missionaries," suggest it; on the contrary, true indigenization takes place only because the "indigenous" church has itself become truly missionary, with or without the blessing of the "missionaries."(96)

To indigenize, Von Allmen called for missionaries, translators and poets who could best preach, translate concepts, and be imaginative in cross-cultural conceptualization of the gospel. (97) Theology was not a relevant synthesis of the right modern components, but rather a more traditionally pictured school in two parts: critical and systematic. (98)

Von Allmen is considered a popular contextualizer more because of what he is not than what he is. He is not a technical contextualizer. Nor does he share the beliefs of the evangelicals, although much of what he advocated in this article is consonant with their beliefs. Thus he placed with many strange bedfellows into the group of popular contextualizers. (99)

4

An Evangelical Approach: Context-Indigenization

Those among evangelical ranks who have searched for a definition of the term contextualization have usually gone to the
words of the Theological Education Fund. These words have
been encountered above but are worthy of review and are included herein for the reader's convenience.

> It [contextualization] means all that is
> implied in the familiar term "indigeniza-
> tion" and yet seeks to press beyond. Con-
> textualization has to do with how we as-
> sess the peculiarity of third world con-
> texts. Indigenization tends to be used in
> the sense of responding to the Gospel in
> terms of a traditional culture. Context-
> ualization, while not ignoring this, takes
> into account the process of secularity,
> technology, and the struggle for human
> justice, which characterizes the histori-
> cal moment of nations in the Third World.(1)

What was meant behind these words, in terms of technical
contextualization, has been discussed. When evangelicals
have encountered this passage, their interpretation has run
distinctly differently. Indigenization to them has meant
communicating the gospel and fitting it to the culture.
"Contextualization" to evangelicals, taking their "lead"
from TEF, has meant utilizing patterns of indigenization
and grappling with new influences in modern culture. This
was the popular understanding at the First Trinity Consultation on Theology and Missions at Trinity Evangelical Divinity

Evangelical Divinity School, 22-25 March 1976. In the discussion group assigned to the topic of contextualization,
discussants were very concerned about adjusting to the new
situation found worldwide. Indigenization appeared to be a
narrower historical concept that dealt basically with
"static" traditional patterns and religions. Thus, they
sought to press beyond and deal with modern life. They considered important the deep-seated cultural patterns, but
looked also to deal with new cultural overlays such as
secularism, Marxism and the many other new currents abroad.

To them, there was no thought of contextualizing in the
technical or popular sense wherein *context becomes part of
the content*, and analyses of the situation often serve as
excuses by which to import radical ideologies and theologies.
The historical indigenous principles were still assumed.
And it seemed a proper process, and in accord with the TEF,
considering that TEF had written, "It means all that is implied in. . . 'indigenization.'"

The situation had been basically the same at the 1975
Evangelical Foreign Missions Association Executives Retreat.
What the group called "contextualization" clearly fell in
the category of indigenization.(2) Seeking to explain the
scope of "contextualization," they decided to divide it into
two categories: ". . . first, seeking for a correctly *applied* [emphasis mine] theology which avoids the dangers of
syncretism, and second, *applying* it to the current problems
of our times."(3) Applied theology, however, was what the
TEF was seeking to move away from. To them, a theology that
had to be applied was by that basic fact already irrelevant.
To them a contextualized theology did not need "applying"
because it was drawn from the context.

For these basic reasons, and for deeper reasons, it seems
highly inappropriate to label the evangelical efforts as
"contextualization." Their work is better labeled as
"context-indigenization," meaning the indigenizing of the
gospel in the modern context. This term truly means all
that is meant in the traditional understanding of the term
indigenization. Yet it seeks to press beyond it by imple-
menting insights of anthropology, among other things. At
the same time, however, these insights are subjected to the
judgment of Scripture.

A statement written by the dean of the evangelical Yeotmal
Seminary in India is significant for what it almost says
compared to what it means. Athyal wrote: ". . . true

theology should maintain a healthy *balance* between belonging
to God and his Word, and at the same time belonging to the
contemporary world, that is, between its uniqueness and its
relevance."(4) Athyal almost says that a *dialectic* should
be maintained between God and his Word on the one hand, and
the contemporary world in the sense practiced by technical
contextualizers on the other hand. But what is meant is al-
together different.

The full context of the Athyal quote must be considered.
He does not advocate technical contextualization. In fact,
he repudiates the work of unnamed popular contextualizers:

> Any theology, to be meaningful and rele-
> vant, should be a "contextual theology."
> But the danger of several Asian Christian
> thinkers is their over-enthusiasm in pre-
> ferring the "context" to the hard core of
> Christianity, namely the historical Christ
> and the Gospel, as seen in the "text."
> The text points to God's self-revelation
> in a unique and absolute way in history;
> the context is only the vehicle of under-
> standing that. The former represents the
> "theos" part, the latter the "logos" part
> of "theo-logy." And· true theology should
> maintain a healthy balance. . .(5)

This healthy balance is envisioned by the context-
indigenizers and depends first of all on an equal weighting
of each point. The "hard-core" as envisioned by Athyal is
virtually non-existent in any developed form in the thought
or at least in the products of the contextualizers. It
should become ever clearer that the grouping envisioned in
this book between contextualizers and indigenizers is wider
than just the areas of context and culture. Basic theological presuppositions, methodologies and affinities are involved. Contextualization or context-indigenization are
just the missiological methodologies of these deeper elements.

The Bangkok '73 conference on "Salvation Today," sponsored
by the Commission on World Mission and Evangelism of the
World Council of Churches was contemporaneous with the introduction of the contextualization thrust. Peter Beyerhaus
in his book on the conference(6) discussed a division that
is strikingly parallel to the group roughly outlined above.
He went beyond the standard grouping of the "two-views--
namely, proponents of the biblical testimony and those who

focused on the concrete situations of the recipients of the message. . . ."(7)

> The *first* group took its point of depar-
> ture essentially from the statements of
> Holy Scripture which it saw as the direct-
> ing and normative authority also for the
> attainment of salvation today. The *se-
> cond* group was already so deeply engaged
> in political and social efforts to change
> modern society that it was hardly able to
> muster time or interest for the study of
> Scripture. This group even called into
> question the place of personal faith in
> Jesus Christ as an indispensable pre-
> requisite for salvation. Finally, a
> *third* group was made up of the practi-
> tioners of modern biblical scholarship
> and in particular those who stressed a
> historical-critical methodology.(8)

The groupings made by Beyerhaus can be roughly related
to the contextualization continuum as follows: His *first*
with context-indigenizers; his *second* with technical contextualizers; his *third* with popular contextualizers.(9)
Beyerhaus's expansion of the traditional two-group division
is helpful, providing greater insight into the contextualization scene. And yet the two-fold division holds true, too,
in that neither of the proponent groups of contextualization
holds to a view of Scripture making it the "hard core" as
does Athyal, or in which it is held as "the directing and
normative authority," as in Beyerhaus.

Theology--An Attempt at Definition

The theological premises of technical contextual theology
contrast sharply with the traditional bases of theology. It
will be helpful to consider these at this point in order to
show more clearly what contextualization is not, and into
what context-indigenization sinks its roots.

Orlando Costas stated the position of the theology of
liberation, a school closely related to the technical
contextualization group, as follows:

> . . . the theology of liberation breaks
> with the theologies of the North Atlantic
> at the level of the tools it employs.

> Theology as a critical reflection on the
> praxis of faith is preceded by previous
> analysis of the sociopolitical reality.
> This means that its primary tools are
> those of the social sciences, for they
> have the first word with respect to the
> concrete data of the historical praxis.(10)

Traditional theology,(11) and modern evangelical theology,
for the most part, would shudder at such a subjective approach to theology. Evangelical theologians would agree
with Peter Berger's emphasis on the importance of placing
any theology in a framework, not an ideological one, but an
historical and doctrinal framework. He wrote, "The fundamental questions of theology have been passionately considered
for at least three thousand years. It is. . . insufferable
arrogance to think that one can begin theology in sovereign
disregard of this history. . ."(12)

Traditional theology throughout history has not taken
praxis as its starting point. Rather it has, to varying
degrees, been derived from and nurtured on the Bible.(13)
Martin Luther refined the process to conscious use of *sola
scriptura*. Pinnock reiterated the dictum in 1971. "*Sola
scriptura* is the *Protestant principle*. *Scripture* consti-
tutes, determines and rules the entire theolgoical endeavor.
What it does not determine is no part of Christian truth."(14)
Hodge claimed that the theologians' "only proper course" was
to derive his theology from the Bible.(15) These truths so
derived were assumed to come from an *integrated* source--the
Bible. This view is contrary to the view held by non-
evangelicals who see distinct and even contradictory theologies plualistically contained in the Bible. It follows
that the position one holds on Scripture will be reflected
in all theologizing. Pluralists look for a rainbow of paral-
leling and various theological themes and fragments. Evangelicals and their forebears hold to a unified Bible.

Hodge proposed "to take these facts of Scripture, determine their relation to each other and to further cognate
truths, as well as to vindicate them and show their *harmony*
and *consistency* [emphasis mine]."(16)

A. H. Strong held a view similar to Hodge. To him the
aim of theology was "the ascertainment of the facts representing God and the relations between God and the universe,
and the exhibition of these facts in their rational unity

as connected parts of a formulated and organic system of truth."(17)

Not only was the Bible considered a non-contradictory source of inter-related truth but the basic evangelical position has been anchored firmly in the belief in an infallible, inerrant Bible. The study group on the authority and uniqueness of Scripture at the International Congress on World Evangelization reported their finding that belief in an "inerrant Bible" designates "the entire trustworthiness of all Scripture says, without exception." "At the same time," they noted, "Scripture must be interpreted fairly in accord with what each passage in context is really endeavoring to affirm." (18) This idea is not new, of course. It was propagated in the Bible itself, from the many instances of "and God said" found in Leviticus, to II Timothy 3:16. One of the most masterful expositions on the inspiration and unity of the Bible was L. Gaussen's *Theopneustia: The Bible, Its Divine Origin and Entire Inspiration, Deduced from Internal Evidence and the Testimonies of Nature, History, and Science*, first published in 1841 in Edinburgh, Scotland. In a comment related to the issue of plural theologies in the Bible Gaussen wrote: "Let it not be imagined, then, that the stamp of the individual character of the sacred writers in the several books of the Bible, authorizes us to regard their inspiration as intermittent or incomplete."(19)

The Core

Those who encounter evangelical discussion on "the core" may be tempted to equate this with theories such as the modern thoughts which have been built on C. H. Dodd's teaching on *kerygma*.(20) The two cannot be equated, however. When evangelicals emphasize certain doctrines or place them in "the core," they are not suggesting a methodology which elevates certain themes over others. Rather such statements usually stand as an evangelical assumption of the primacy of, or allow as the only premise, the Bible. The methodology implemented is generally induction from the authoritative Scriptures understood in historical context, or historical-grammatical exegesis. Non-evangelical method implies distilled reflection on a praxis,(21) among other things.

Although there is important agreement on these issues among context-indigenizers, there also is disagreement as to the nature and extent or content of "the core."(22) In a significant consultation related to the matter, among

participants Alan R. Tippett, Donald A. McGavran, J. C.
Hoekendijk and Peter Beyerhaus on "Christopaganism or Indigenous Christianity?" Donald McGavran suggested a content
for "the core." His three-part core included (1) "belief in
and allegiance to the Triune God only"; (2) "belief in the
Bible as the only inspired Word of God, the infallible rule
of faith and practice"; and (3) belief in "those great central facts, commands, ordinances and doctrines which are so
clearly set forth in the Bible." To McGavran, "Anything
which damages this core is forbidden syncretism."(23)

As one surveys the writings of evangelicals on this matter there are many stated or implied formulations of "the
core." Saphir Athyal suggested the core as "the historical
Christ and the Gospel as seen in the 'text.'"(24) Not every-
one was seen as able to do this type of theological formulating. Pieper held that "There is no *theologia irregenitorum*."
(25) Thus, evangelical theology must be done by one who has
been spiritually reborn, who accepts the whole Bible as his
supreme authority as perceived according to the leading of
the Holy Spirit who indwells him. Perhaps, while not ignoring the questions of what to emphasize first, it might be
suggested that *the Bible itself* is understood as "the core"
out of which various key doctrines are to be emphasized. In
all, the relationship with and emphasis on the living Christ
is to be paramount, with His Word and its application being
the theologian's prime concern here on earth.

These basics, rightly extrapolated, must lead to the possibility of heresy. Any unregenerate "theologian" must be
assumed to be a ready source for various heresies.(26) And
deviations from or contradictions of God's truth in the
Bible must be considered "un-truth" and therefore heretical
and anathema. Clark Pinnock asserted, "It is our duty to be
faithful to truth and intolerant of error."(27) Such an attitude is hard to reconcile with tolerant plualism that accepts insights of praxis that sharply contort the natural
sense of various Biblical teachings. This is another reason
why evangelicals must be classed wholly apart from the contextualizers.

Two Different Roots Produce Two Different Fruits

The influence of one's view of Scripture must be herein
pursued more completely. In Chapter I the contextualization
diagrams illustrated to what extent the Bible, when viewed
through the higher-critical and modern confessional grids,
influenced one's theology.(28) This was then subjected to a

dialectical process in interaction with strongly weighted
socio-political analysis. Both the thesis, "dogmatic" theology, and the antithesis, the context, were informed from
other sources. Radical and neo-orthodox hermeneutics and
their accompanying emphases influenced theology. A political and ideological-religious "framework" determined the
evaluation and use of cultural fragments. These included
the restricted number of biblical motifs advocated by political theology and also the influence of Marxism. Maoism in
China impressed contextualizers, who held to a "new man"
theology and searched for the Word of the cosmic Christ.(29)
A third element, that of dialogue, also entered the synthe-
sizing process. Universalism, and the belief that the cosmic Christ speaks clearly to all men, were added to the positive contributions to Christianity it was expected that dialogue might bring. Synthesis was to produce a freshly contextualized theology. This in turn would be validated by
praxis.(30)

This illustration does not go far enough, however. For
it assumes that one always deals with "antiquated" and often
Bible-based dogmatics. More realistically, in technical
contextualization such a spot would next be filled with the
contextualized theology. This theology would then interact
with context and living faiths resulting in a new synthesis.
And so the process would continue(31) (see Figures 4 and 5).

The evangelical methodology takes the form of belief in
an authoritative and inerrant Scripture which provides content and basic categories for theology. For example, one's
view of man's nature would be drawn primarily from the Bible.
This occurs in a step-by-step process as the principles of
historical-grammatical exegesis are applied and then developed into biblical theology, and then systematic theology.
(32) From these grow more specialized theologies, such as
theology of missions and evangelism. Finally, from this
missiology comes principles and practices, in Figure 6, mission principles and practices. Context-indigenization occurs in levels two through six.(33) Contextualization of
theology is both a missiological directive and a fundamental
theological belief. The whole schematization (Figure 6)
hardly relates to technical or even popular contextualization.(34)

The basic differences in the systems, namely, the dialectic versus the deliberately biblically based one, can be
seen in the way they work themselves out. For instance, in
evangelistic method, they are quite different.

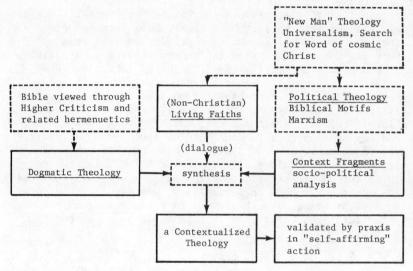

Figure 4: the technical contextualization process in its early stage. The three boxes interact to form a contextualized theology. These three factors were influenced by the beliefs, philosophies and practices shown in the dotted boxes. For example, the search for the word of the cosmic Christ had led radical theologians and some liberals to locate God's Word in non-Christian religions. Thus the connecting line showing this relationship. Such a belief also led to the locating of God's Word in Marxism. This belief influenced the development of political theology which influenced the ordering of context fragments.

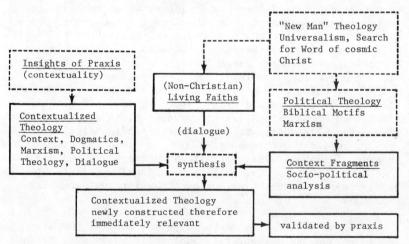

Figure 5: technical contextualization as it works itself out in later practice. Note how dogmatic theology has been "updated." The new contextualized theology, whose content includes the fruits of dialogue and Marxism among other thoughts, then meets with new contexts and in fresh dialogue to produce a further contextualized theology. Each time the process recycles, influence of dogmatic theology lessens proportionately.

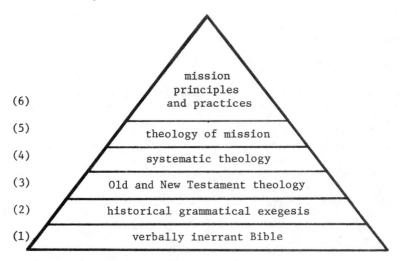

mission
principles
and practices

(6)

(5) theology of mission

(4) systematic theology

(3) Old and New Testament theology

(2) historical grammatical exegesis

(1) verbally inerrant Bible

Figure 6: a traditional schematization of evangelical theology

Contextualizers advocate a witness of praxis and dialogue and reject or downplay talk of "saving souls."(35) Context-indigenizers talk of communication, sowing, reaping and nurturing.(36) Contextualizers often mix the church with the world,(37) whereas context-indigenizers specifically seek to plant, build and strengthen the church.(38) Contextualization advocates see culture as benign or bearing God's revelatory imprint. Context-indigenizers, although seeing the good, believe in the fallen nature of man and see this reflected in his cultures.(39) The work of both thus turns out to be quite different. While representatives of either might be found feeding the hungry, basically the contextualizers might be engaged in dialogue or in arming revolutionaries, while the great majority of church planters and radio preachers may be found in the evangelical ranks.

Communicating the Core in Awareness

Those who work to bring the gospel to modern man are now equipped with many tools. For example, since World War II there has been a noticeable increase in anthropological training for evangelical missionaries. Those who fault modern missionaries often are speaking of past mistakes.

Prior to World War II much great missionary work was done. Many lasting results were available for informed observers to note. Some scars from the mistakes were also evident.(40) For example, in the first half of the nineteenth century Adoniram Judson had conscientously worked and studied as a missionary in Burma.(41) He translated the Bible. He studied many classical Burmese works. From them he learned not only a rich and technical vocabulary but also the lilt and feel of the language and the people. Yet he refused to translate the Buddhist holy works into the common tongue of those non-Buddhists among whom he most largely worked, nor into modern European languages, because he felt them to be distractions from God's Word and a great waste of his translating skills and time. Many followed his example, although not always with the discernment or discretion of Judson. Cultural forms and practices were at times unequivocally scored by some missionaries. Some believers became newly acculturated members of foreign islands in the culture of their birth.(42)

Many ways of taking the culture into account have been developed since Judson's days. Contextualization and context-indigenization are but the most recent of many. Some of the practices developed have been termed "adaptation," "accommodation," "*possessio*," "reinterpretation," "restructuring," "reformulation," and "conceptualization" as well as the larger term "indigenization." There were other methods too.(43)

Saphir Athyal called the "over-enthusiasm" of several Asian Christian thinkers a danger when they preferred "the 'context' to the hard core of Christianity. . ." This appears to be a reaction against the contextualizers. He suggested that the context is only the vehicle of understanding the Bible. It is true that all peoples have contextual configurations by which they perceive all things. (44) These configurations and the prejudices attached to them are of concern to context-indigenizers because use, or misuse, of them will greatly affect communication of the core. When discussing contextualization, Byang Kato really talked about the issues relevant to context-indigenization, namely communication and content problems. He saw "contextualization" as "an effort to express the *never changing* [emphasis mine] Word of God in ever-changing modes for relevance. Since the Gospel message is inspired but the mode of its expression is not, contextualization of *the modes of expression* is not only right but necessary."(45)

It is at this point that Kato, the technical contextualizers and the Lausanne discussants on the topic of hermeneutics all turned to the incarnation. The technical contextualizers suggested that Christ incarnated God's Word.
In just the same way, they held, we today must incarnate
God's active Word among the nations. Evangelical emphasis
has sounded quite similar (or perhaps ecumenical actions are
labeled with the same term as the actions and beliefs of the
evangelicals), yet has been quite dissimilar.(46)

Saphir Athyal, in this case discussing hermeneutics at
Lausanne '74, likened the incarnation of Christ, the Word,
to the inscripturation of the Bible, the Word.(47) Both,
he pointed out, were Truth dressed up in the cultural cloth-
ing of the contemporary context. But then, instead of continuing the analogy and advocating modern incarnated Christians revealing God's new Word for today, he talked of ways
of communicating *that truth*. This communication process has
been described by Dr. David J. Hesselgrave of Trinity Evangelical Divinity School as a man standing on a mountain
ridge. Looking into the valley ahead of him, he tries to
describe it to those in the valley behind him, in approxi-
mate, and relative terms relevant to their understanding.(48)
To be communicated, in this illustration, is a specific body
of knowledge: a given amount of truth. Yet that truth is
definitely influenced by the culture into which it is going.
In this communication process the purpose is to make the
information to be communicated "relevant in every situation
everywhere as long as the Gospel is not compromised."(49)

Indigenization of the Gospel

When one departs from specific analysis of the contextualization process as advocated especially by the technical
contextualizers, one moves from a specific, dialectically
and politically minded school of thought into the large
world of "history of hermeneutics." For the communication
of a perceived core, from the inscripturating culture through
the grid of the exegete and into the receiving culture, can
most clearly be traced along with the historical development
of hermeneutics. Various theories have abounded through
time and many exist today.(50)

H. Richard Niebuhr in his book *Christ and Culture* provided
an alternative way of grouping gospel-to-culture approaches.
(51) His first type was Christ-against-culture or the
counterculture approach.(52) Examples of this approach include approaches illustrated in Tertullian, medieval

Monasticism, Anabaptism, Tolstoy, and some modern groups.(53)
His second type was called Christ-of-culture, which could
also be called the accommodationist approach. Representatives of this approach include Abelard, the Gnostics, some
Protestant liberals--Schliermacher, Ritschl and others, and
perhaps even Louis Luzbetak.(54) Christ-above-culture, the
synthesist approach, was practiced by the second century
apologists Justin Martyr and Clement of Alexandria, and by
St. Thomas Aquinas, Pope Leo XIII and others. The dualist
approach, or Christ-and-culture-in-paradox, was taken by
Luther, Kierkegaard, Troeltsch and others. Augustine, Calvin
and F. D. Maurice were major practitioners of the conversionist model or Christ-the-Transformer-of-culture.

Various Scriptural references have been adduced in support of the above positions. Notably, Paul was labeled as
most dualist, and John as conversionist. Various sources
have been used to support the Christ-against-culture position.

As one considers how Christ affects culture, the corresponding matter of how culture affects Christianity is a
topic about which numerous books and articles have been
written. The many related anthropological researches and
findings are beyond the scope of this paper, but germane to
the discussion is the question of whether or not there are
unacceptable adaptations that might be made in the indigenization process. When determined, these must be considered
as syncretism.(55)

Although Christianity must be a life-giving and life-
changing force in a culture, it does not necessarily have to
be a foreign element in the sense of being identified with
another *human* culture. The gospel must be recognizable to
the people within their cultural matrices. Linguists have
recognized this fact. Although exactly corresponding terms
are rarely, if ever, available, linguists have come to look
for dynamic equivalents.(56) Those in the receiving cultures who have had the opportunity to speak out have also
called for dynamic equivalency in other areas. These concerns include ecclesiology, music, and art.(57)

Even the basic situation of local autonomy and leadership
which is related to one's ecclesiology must be considered.
From the time when Titus was told to appoint local bishops,
to the work of Cyril and Methodius who in the ninth century
translated the liturgy into the local vernacular, much work
has been done to make the church "at home."(58) One notable

missiological school of thought has been the Three-Self
Movement. This harks back to the pioneering work of John L.
Nevius and the Korean Church. The concerns of the Navius
Method are well illustrated in the statement of it:

> 1. To let each man abide in the calling
> wherein he was found, teaching that each
> was to be an individual worker for Christ
> in his own neighborhood, supporting him-
> self by his trade.
>
> 2. To develop church methods and machin-
> ery only so far as the native church was
> able to take care of and manage them.
>
> 3. So far as the church itself was able
> to provide the men and the means, to set
> aside the better qualified to do evangel-
> istic work among their neighbors.
>
> 4. To let the natives provide their own
> church buildings, which were to be *native
> in architecture* [emphasis mine] and of
> such style as the local church could af-
> ford to put up.(59)

The basic formula for the approach had three elements:
(1) self-government; (2) self-support; and (3) self-
propagation. The method was extremely successful in Korea
and in other mission fields. As it was implemented, native
church architecture took shape, local tunes were appropriated for Christian hymnody, believers learned the joys of
Christian stewardship and the exhilaration of spiritual re-
production. Those who have assessed the movement in retro-
spect have noted that *missionary emphasis* by the local church
to distant parts of the world was lacking from the three-
self movement and made the planted churches "self-ish."
Self-formulation was often lacking, too, as training of
leadership lagged woefully behind the ingathering of the new
believers. Theological systems, methods of preaching, and
teaching were often in the imported style. Important areas
of teaching were neglected.

For example, power politics in the spiritual realm has
been pointed out by Jahnheinz Jahn(60) as an important point
to consider in many African societies. The same has proven
true in Latin America. In one area, because group leaders
had not been fully trained and because of a calculated over-
sight on the missionaries' part, the local believers were not

taught of the *power* of the Spirit of God, an important point
to people who were embattled by lesser spirits. For them,
the gospel which they had received in North American form
needed to be put into their context.(61)

If a person from such a tribal background moved to town
at age 10 and grew up as a city person, his context would be
more complex. Issues such as disintegration of extended
family ties and the morality connected to such a system, or
ethics related to bribery by expatriate officials of multi-
national corporations would also plague this person. For
him the gospel would need to speak to his problems. In a
sense it would need to be indigenized. More specifically,
in this modern urban scene it would need context-indigenization.

Indigenization According to the TEF

It has already been shown that "contextualization" as defined implies that *context* in some way becomes part of the
content of the Word. In technical contextualization this
means importation of ideology into content. In popular
contextualization this means contextual fragments and insights become part of the content of the Word.

TEF's conceptualization of indigenization is crucial in
understanding how contextualization developed in contrast
to evangelical development of the indigenization process.
Several sentences from *Ministry in Context* will serve to
illustrate briefly: "Indigenization tends to be used in
the sense of *responding to* [emphasis mine] the Gospel in
terms of a traditional culture." Having already stated that
contextualization "seeks to press beyond" indigenization,
authentic contextualization was seen as "arising out of a
genuine encounter between God's word and *His* [emphasis mine]
world. . ."(62)

The unique wording of the passage is troublesome when
seen through an evangelical grid. There, indigenization is
roughly defined to mean "putting the gospel into." Talk of
"responding to" seems backwards. Actually this reflects
well the contextualization thrust wherein context affects
content. In defining indigenization, TEF appears to have
failed to distinguish content from form. Or to put it another way, in their indigenizing, culture and context are
allowed to severely manipulate the text.(63) That this observation is to the point may be observed as TEF in the same
passage delineated "false contextualization" wherein too
much manipulation and cultural intrusion resulted in "culture

faith." It may be correctly assumed that the "right amount" of cultural intrusion made for "good indigenization." Thus, in the contextualization process, refilling the content with context might have seemed only a natural continuation of indigenization so conceived.

Context-Indigenization Subdivided

Terms are loosely defined in the literature on context-indigenization, making comparison and correlation difficult. To facilitate discussion, a tentative grouping is herein set forth. It is suggested that most of the literature may be roughly fitted into one or another of the proposed categories.

Dr. James O. Buswell III, visiting professor in anthropology at Trinity Evangelical Divinity School, proposed a division of evangelical contextualization (or context-indigenization).(64) He suggested three areas: (1) inculturation, (2) indigenization and (3) ethnotheology.(65) Other groupings have been suggested,(66) but these often have overlapping or contradictory elements and do not aid in discussion of contextualization of theology. It will be seen upon further investigation of these three categories that all have to do to some degree with theology. This theology brings with it a demand of things to be added to culture, and finds elements of culture to be judged and rejected, modified, or adapted.

Context-Indigenization of the Word: Inculturation

In the *evangelism* stage in any cross-cultural witness there is that interaction which Professor G. Linwood Barney of the Alliance School of Theology and Mission has called "inculturation." The process as defined by him does not deal fully with all the processes involved at this "stage one" of context-indigenization, but it will serve well as a cover term. Inculturation can be described basically as "disengaging the supracultural elements of the Gospel from one culture to another and 'contextualizing' them within the cultural forms and social institutions of another, with at least some degree of transformation of those forms and institutions. . ."(67)

Dr. J. Herbert Kane suggests that theology can be divided into (1) that which God knows about Himself and His will, or Absolute Theology,(68) (2) that which has been revealed by Christ and all that is in the Bible, or Revealed Theology,(69) and (3) that part of truth that each theologian makes his own, or Partial Theology.(70) This last would reflect enculturation of the theologian himself and would be in a very real sense indigenous. Under this scheme, then, those cultural elements in Partial Theology would have to be disengaged from Revealed Theology and a new culturally relevant Partial Theology be constructed when the gospel is taken from one culture to another.

G. Linwood Barney speaks in somewhat parallel terms of (1) the supracultural absolutes, (2) constants and (3) cultural relativities.(71) Explaining his position Barney wrote:

> God is absolute, underived and unchanging.
> But consider the following implications.
> The Gospel is given of God. Therefore it
> is derived. It cannot be absolute. Is it
> therefore relative? If so, it is change-
> able. Yet Paul (Galatians) speaks of the
> one Gospel. We need another conceptual
> category between absolute and relative.
> It would seem that the term "constant"
> might meet this need. Constant refers to
> that which, by nature, does not change
> though it may be derived. . . Then it fol-
> lows, God is absolute. That which he ini-
> tiates and affirms to man in his covenant
> and redeeming acts is constant; however,
> the forms in which man responds to God are
> tied to his culture and therefore are
> relative. The absolute *and the constant*
> *are supracultural* [emphasis mine] but
> man's response is relative and thus can
> vary from culture to culture as each so-
> ciety expresses the supracultural in forms
> peculiar to its own cultural configuration.
> Thus a relevant expression of the God-man
> relationship can preserve the integrity of
> a culture but in no way needs to compro-
> mise the essence and nature of the supra-
> cultural.(72)

Speaking of this whole process of the gospel engaging it-self in a culture, Buswell has suggested that most who hold to an authoritative Word work with basically the same model as that described by Barney.(73)

Subdividing the inculturation process of Partial Theologizing, one finds, among others, the activities of translation, evangelism, apologetics and preaching. In these, an informal theology is presented which is not as systematic as ethnotheology. Such a theology, however, contains in germinal form the broad outlines of a mature systematic. Thus, what is perceived by the new convert as the implications of his newly embraced faith will prove to be quite profound and are therefore significant.(74)

Since inculturation is the first step in the context-indigenization process, its activities must be tentative and exploratory whenever a new culture is encountered. As steps two and three come into play the elements of inculturation are refined.(75)

For example, evangelistic method may be considered.(76) When missionaries first encountered a culture, the first step was translation, if necessary. In the process, local examples of redemption analogies were often observed.(77) These examples illustrating God's redemptive call to repentance and forgiveness became part of an informal ethnotheology. Preaching illustrations and apologetics(78) were somewhat primitive attempts to relate the culture to the gospel. The transcultural nature of the biblical cultures often proved a help in communicating. And in the process the Holy Spirit also worked to bring the hearer to understanding and repentance.

The process of inculturating the method of evangelism is especially necessary. Not only do methods vary in effectiveness from culture to culture, but also from time to time in any given culture.(79)

The culture also determines principles and practices of the communication process itself. Addressing the concerns of the people will heighten the possibility of effective communication. And the transmitting of the message from person to person will follow the natural routes of the culture. Taking a lead from McGavran, George Peters in a discussion on psycho-socio-cultural factors in evangelism wrote:

> . . . the effectiveness of evangelism
> depends upon our ability to design and
> apply methods of evangelism that will
> integrate and utilize the social web of
> relationships of people as natural

> "bridges of God" between individuals,
> families, tribes, and communities. Such
> relationships serve most effectively as
> channels for the flow of dynamics in
> evangelism and Gospel expansion.(80)

A quite well known mass evangelism approach is evangelism-in-depth. This represents a context-indigenized form of evangelism representing the work of ethnotheologists, formal or informal, who are members of the indigenous church. (81) The result is a methodology refined and informed by a maturing ethnotheology.(82)

Another area must also be considered in the inculturation stage. And that is judgment. As Christians endeavor to bring the Word of God to people in a new culture, some initial judgments must be carefully made. Some cultural practices, such as suttee, cannot wait for the careful evaluation of indigenous Christian ethnotheologians. Infanticide, though deeply related and rooted in a culture, must be condemned by those who love and serve the Lord Jesus Christ.(83) Thus rejection is one aspect of judgment that must be implemented in the initial context-indigenization phase. This judgment also involves acceptance and incorporation or modification of various themes and mores.(84) Judson, whose missionary judgments were referred to earlier, adopted the cultural role of "teacher" in Burma. He dressed like a teacher, built himself a structure peculiar to teaching, and adopted the title of teacher. All was done with an eye to evangelism as he adopted, modified or transformed cultural elements. Those who were converted adopted many of these elements into their indigenous Christianity. Which leads us to the second major phase of context-indigenization.

Context-indigenization of the Church and its Leadership: Indigenization

The principles of the early missiologists Venn, Nevius and Allen constitute a significant part of this process.(85) This is a process encountered after the first convert is won, and one which extends throughout the life of the church as local Christians are discipled and nurtured, either by the local Christians or by the missionary.

Calling this the "indigenization" stage,(86) Buswell suggested that such a process occurs best in Christian homes of the culture. At this stage the tentative inculturation process becomes natural enculturation. Buswell wrote,

> When the Christian home rears its child-
> ren as Christians and the teachings and
> belief system of Christ is "born or pro-
> duced within" the home, Christianity is
> *indigenous* within that culture. Then
> the Christianity thus established need
> not be thought of as tied to any parti-
> cular traditions of the past. It becomes
> a part of the society and its culture
> where it is, and may continue to be a
> part of it as it changes. Thus it may be
> as forward-looking as the people who bear
> it.(87)

The contextualizers are concerned, rightly, about rapid social change. Context-indigenization is also equipped to
deal with rapid social change. With mature disciples of
Christ living in the culture and subject to the changes of
it, a solid base is laid for dealing with the opportunities
that arise and are opened by the Holy Spirit. Such Christians can be salt and light to the glory of God.(88)

Those who, in 1977, held the triennial meeting of the Association of Evangelicals of Africa and Madagascar (AEAM) ob-
viously agreed with this emphasis. Their conference theme
was on the Christian home in Africa. The program emphasized
personal relationships with Christ as Savior and Lord. Family relationships were to be infused with the fruits of the
Spirit. Christians in Africa were then to change the context around them moving out as God's people, and were to be
validated as such by their relationship with Christ and by
their godly homelife.(89)

Patterns and forms of institutionalized Christianity fit
into the category of context-indigenization of the church.
Church architecture, liturgy, vestments, hymnody, art, order
of service, ceremonies and the like all come to be "at home"
in this stage.

People movements, wherein large segments of the populace
turn to Christ, may occur at this stage in close conjunction
with inculturation work and ethnotheology. In all, the goal
is a cultural and ecclesiastical type of "dynamic equivalence"
(90) in which the church comes to "have the same meaning and
function within the culture as the early church had for the
people in the culture of that time."(91)

Context-indigenization of the Word
by the Church: Ethnotheology

Stephen Knapp criticized ethnotheology as falling short
of meeting the issues raised by the contextualizers. Statements on justice, politics and economics are lacking in a
context-indigenization process, he charged.(92) Yet as he
too struggled against what he considered the unacceptable
methodology and content of technical and popular contextualization and tried to formulate an evangelical alternative, it
seems to this writer, that he only developed a more comprehensive ethnotheology.(93)

The term must be defined before any further discussion is
attempted. Again we turn to Buswell. To him ethnotheology
is:

> . . . theology done from inside the system,
> rendering the supracultural Christian abso-
> lutes not only in the linguistic idiom but
> also within the particular forms that "sy-
> stem" takes within the system: concepts
> of priority, sequence, time,(94) space;
> elements of order, customs of validation
> and assertion; styles of emphasis and ex-
> pression.(95)

It appears that Buswell borrowed the term "ethnotheology"
from an article by Charles Kraft of Fuller Seminary. Kraft
used his term to denote a new discipline which combines the
best from Systematic Theology and from Anthropology.(96)
Buswell envisioned ethnotheology in a more general way. To
him it appears to mean a systematic theology done by Christians within a culture. Thus ethno-theology is theology of
the *ethne*. This has been the general meaning of the term as
used in this book as well.

To posit an ethnotheology is not to automatically place
oneself in support of a pluralistic rainbow of distinct
theologies. It must be remembered that the Bible remains
the authoritative and sufficient source of theology for all
cultures and subcultures. But those of different cultures
do come to the text with different questions.

A theology of crisis is appropriate to each ethnotheology.
This has to do with the Christian view on rites of passage
as practiced by the culture. A Christianity that does not
tell converts how they should react when an infant falls ill

is deficient in ethnotheology. Rather than resorting to
traditional "medicines" or modern "despairs" an understood,
contextually indigenized gospel would provide aid and succor for such distressed persons.(97)

When linearly-oriented prophetic Christianity faces a
cyclic time concept in the Orient, ethnotheology comes into
play as conceptual gaps are bridged and converts are led to
see the truth of the biblical view of time. Koyama suggested
that the wrath of God, a reaction rooted in time, might help
to bridge such a gap. The reality that God answers prayer,
in time, that he leads even unregenerate people as they come
to himself and that as a shepherd he is constantly urging,
guiding or perhaps chastening his people, helps those in
fast-changing cultures to realize that God is able to move
just as quickly as they and their surroundings.

An ethnotheology even must take into account "framework."
A.O. Dyson struggled with this question. The contextualizers
came up with an ideological and transcultural framework and
methodology. Context-indigenization is to work with the
supracultural, the transcultural and the cultural in considering framework. A synthesis of such patterns results
in a systematic *ethne* theology. Supracultural framework is
contained within the Bible. Its major themes, doctrines,
and commands must be incorporated into all ethnotheologies.
(98) Transcultural framework may be appropriated. These
include lessons learned through history.(99) Up to this
point all ethnotheologies would be very similar.(100) Cultural frameworks would determine the sequence and prioritiz-
ing of such doctrines and might add new themes to the transcultural deposit(101) (Figures 7 and 8).

For example, in this day when occult practices are common in the American-European countries, insights gleaned
from such open spiritual combat in Asia and Africa would be
very helpful to the American churches. Any contextually indigenized ethnotheology would develop full-blown statements
on such issues. Other areas not developed in historic theologies to varying degrees have been polygamy, political and
economic oppression, and justice.

The global village that modern man now lives in is well
suited for cross-fertilization and for exchange of insights.
Travelers in a foreign land often "see" things missed by the
inhabitants. In like manner insights from ethnotheologies
may prove rich and fruitful as they are incorporated into
the transcultural theologies.

```
┌─────────────────────────────────────┐
│          Supracultural Theology      │
│    "the constant," Revealed Theology │
└─────────────────────────────────────┘

                    +

┌─────────────────────────────────────┐
│          Transcultural Theology      │
│          development of doctrine,    │
│      insights from Partial Theologies│
└─────────────────────────────────────┘

                    +

┌─────────────────────────────────────┐
│            Cultural Theology         │
│   Partial Theology: inculturation,   │
│     indigenization, ethnotheology    │
└─────────────────────────────────────┘

                    ↓

┌─────────────────────────────────────┐
│                                      │
│          a Context-Indigenized       │
│                Theology              │
│                                      │
└─────────────────────────────────────┘
```

Figure 7: elements in the context-indigenizing of theology

Ethnotheologies as the result of fully matured context-indigenization also can apply biblical insights to the local *ethne*. Theological judgments first made in the inculturation stage can now be affirmed, modified or refined. Answers can be attempted by theologians from within the local church. To God, is revenge anathema? What about slavery that was so vigorously condemned by the early missionaries? Finer distinctions can be made by these ethnotheologians, as from the position of "insider," questions of bride wealth, pouring of libations, and initiation rites are considered. Quite often the ethnotheologians have been more rigorous in excising the evil than those who, looking from the outside, missed the truly insidious nature of a practice.(102)

It must be suggested that justice be a definite concern of ethnotheology(103) as corporate actions and concerns of the believers are best worked at from the "insider's" viewpoint.

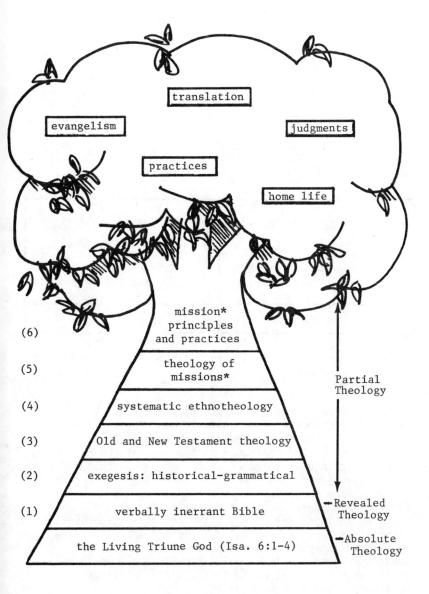

(6)	mission* principles and practices	
(5)	theology of missions*	Partial Theology
(4)	systematic ethnotheology	
(3)	Old and New Testament theology	
(2)	exegesis: historical-grammatical	
(1)	verbally inerrant Bible	Revealed Theology
	the Living Triune God (Isa. 6:1-4)	Absolute Theology

*these could be ecclesiology and church principles, to apply it to another area.

Figure 8: an expanded view of context-indigenization. A fruitful Christianity rooted in God. Phase six shows the branching out into real life of a mature context-indigenized Christianity into interactions and fruitfulness.

Context-indigenization Summarized

The various ways of dealing with context may be charted
as shown in Figure 9. The major distinctions between the
two methodologies are related to the views held of God's
revelation and how closely his Word is to be equated with
the Text. The tools of the technical contextualizers and
the context-indigenizers are distinctly different. The popular contextualizers are a heterogenous group and borrow almost willy nilly from the other approaches.

I. Contextualization	II. Context-indigenization
A. Technical -dialectic B. Popular -incorporation	A. Three major aspects 1. inculturation 2. indigenization 3. ethnotheology
"Content includes Context"	"Supracultural meets full context"

Figure 9: basic elements of the two processes and their
catchwords.

The purpose of these chapters in presenting the analysis
has been to show the broad outlines and distinctives, as
well as the differences between each group. It is the position of this writer that much of the analysis by the contextualizers has shown great skill. However, they construct
approaches upon an unacceptable epistemology and undermine
the authority of Scripture in theologizing. The context-
indigenizers appear to be most true to the will of God as
revealed in those Scriptures. The context-indigenization
methodologies are to be implemented, and all use of the dialectic wherein the Bible and philosophy are equated is to be
shunned. Where possible, and carefully done, it is recom-
mended that insights, not solutions, of the contextualizers
be incorporated into this system.

5
Conclusions

There are several distinct methodologies being practiced by those who are working to bring the gospel into contact with various peoples and cultures of the world. The most recent methodology to gain prominence is contextualization of theology. This term was popularized by the TEF which practiced what, herein, has been termed "technical contextualization."

Technical contextualization has reflected the theological beliefs of its advocates. These beliefs have been identical with, or at least consonant with, radical or political theologies. Basic to the approach is the dialectic, which is employed to assure relevance of theologizing. Various themes of the framework are implemented to give the contextualized fragments a theological meaning. These themes have proven to be theological motifs contained in the political, neo-orthodox and liberal theologies, philosophical views and political formulations. These themes, in effect, give content to the elements of context. The other half of the dialectic is influenced by higher-critical views of the Bible and by dogmatic and confessional theologies. As the process continues, newly contextualized theological formulations influence all further theologizing.

Many now advocate contextualization, but not the technical approach as defined. The non-evangelicals who do so can be classed as "popular contextualizers." These people have not practiced a rigorous dialectic, and some have questioned the findings of political theologies. Their approach, in some cases, includes a greater use of the Bible, and some

seek to communicate and apply Christianity in a way quite
similar to the evangelical approach. The theology of these
people is basically neo-orthodox and liberal. They look for
God's Word to be revealed in places other than, or in addition to, the Bible. Revelation in cognitive statements is
often considered suspect, as they seek to distill God's
"word" from the context, as well as from the text. Both
"words" are then included in their contextualized theology,
along with insights gleaned from Western theologies. Insights discovered in dialogue with other religions are also
appropriated by the popular contextualizers as God's "word."
The result of popular contextualization proves to be a theology touted as relevant, that supplements and supplants biblical teachings with various beliefs, some of them culture-
bound.

Historically, the evangelical approach has been that of
indigenization of the gospel. Many still practice this
method as such. This approach recently, has also been called
contextualization. This, however, appears to be a misuse of
the term, for evangelicals do not contextualize either in
the technical or in the popular way. The main distinction
between evangelical methodology and contextualization is the
high place given to the Bible by evangelicals. The evangelicals implement an informed indigenization. By use of insights gained from anthropology and related social sciences,
and missiology, evangelicals seek to indigenize the gospel
in the modern context. This approach may be termed context-
indigenization.

Implementation of this approach utilizes God's Word, the
Bible, as the source of all theologizing. The practice of
historical-grammatical exegesis in conjunction with context-
indigenization allows the Bible to speak for itself, guard-
ing against the imposition of certain motifs which contra-
dict the teachings of the whole of Scripture.

It seems clear that if evangelicals implement the dialectical approach of technical contextualization, they will deni-
grate the Bible by equating it with something less than God's
special revelation. Technical contextualization is not for
them. Popular contextualization's failure to distinguish
between God's authoritative text and other "words," must
also be avoided by evangelicals as an unnecessary abandon-
ment of God's revelation in an attempt to make His ever-
timely will "relevant." Properly speaking, evangelicals do
not, and should not, contextualize the gospel. The indigenizing, or more properly, the context-indigenizing of the
gospel, should be the method of evangelical work.

Appendices

Appendix A
God in Revolution—Jürgen Moltmann

Thesis 1: We live in a revolutionary situation. In the future we shall experience history more and more as revolution. We can be responsible for the future of man only in a revolutionary way.

Thesis 2: The new revolutionary situation has brought Christianity into a deep crisis of identity. Christians and the churches will rediscover their true self-consciousness only if they overcome their own religious alienation and their own hindrance to the free self-realization of man.

Thesis 3: The eschatological (and messianic) tradition of hope can give rise to a new birth of Christian faith in the revolutionary present.

Thesis 4: The new criterion of theology and faith is to be found in praxis.

Thesis 5: The church is not a heavenly arbiter in the world's strifes. In the present struggles for freedom and justice, Christians must side with the humanity of the oppressed.

Thesis 6: The problem of violence and nonviolence is an illusory problem. There is only the question of the justified and unjustified use of force and the question of whether the means are proportionate to the ends.

Appendix B

A Working Policy for the Implementation of the Third Mandate of the Theological Education Fund

Introduction

Beginning in 1970 the Theological Education Fund was given a new mandate "to help the churches reform the training for the Christian ministry (including the ordained ministry and other forms of Christian leadership in church and world) by providing selective and temporary assistance and consultative services to institutions for theological education and other centres of training."

The determinant goal of its work is that the Gospel be expressed and ministry undertaken in response to:

(a) The widespread crisis of faith,

(b) the issues of social justice and human development,

(c) the dialectic between local cultural and religious situations and a universal technological civilization.

While its main focus is to be on Africa, Asia, the Caribbean, Latin America and the Pacific, it is aware that the questions with which it is dealing are vital for the churches in all six continents. In carrying out the mandate it is authorized to seek $3,300,000 during the period from 1970-1977 when the mandate ends.

Through extensive travel, consultation, survey and study, there have evolved the following plans and policy for the implementation of the mandate.

The Fundamental Stance

The fundamental stance of the TEF during the next five years can only be defined by a series of unavoidable tensions inherent in the task the mandate has laid upon us:

(1) To sense with great clarity that the situation in theological education today demands deep-seated and indeed radical changes in existing aims and structures, and yet to discern what is good and valid from the past. Thus the TEF must develop a program which stands discriminately in continuity with the first two mandate periods, and yet strikes out in new directions in response to the dominating issues before us today. To achieve that kind of sensitivity the basic stance of the TEF must be that of the Servant of Christ, striving to be both priestly and prophetic, both grateful for expressions of responsive faithfulness in the past and hopeful for what is yet to come.

Yet within this position of tension, the TEF program must be weighted toward the demand for change. Throughout much of the Third World (as indeed elsewhere) the basic crisis in theological education can often be traced to the continued dominance of inherited and traditional patterns. The struggle for a more authentic response to the Gospel—to be the servant Church in loco—must overcome the problems imposed by the present crisis in theological education at several key points. Missiologically, the inherited forms may have failed to release the potential of the Gospel as a message of liberation for the poor and oppressed, of liberation of the rich and the poor from the bonds of domination that bind the oppressed and the oppressors, thus falling short of realizing a ministry of the Servant Church. Theologically, both the approach and content of theological reflection tend to move within the framework of Western questions and cultural presuppositions, failing to vigorously address the Gospel of Jesus Christ to the particular situation. Western formulations are sometimes wrongly understood as identical with the universal in Christian theology. Pedagogically, educational methodology developed under the large influence of the inherited patterns, and driven by a demand for highly-trained church leadership, may tend to falsely equate scholasticism with excellence. Structurally, the traditional residential pattern may tend to train people away from those they are to serve, to isolate the process of theological education from the frontier issues of society, while at the same time it is proving to be increasingly unviable financially.

On the whole, therefore, this stance implies clearly that the TEF must concentrate its assistance at those points which promise to come to grips with the widespread demand within the Third World for renewal and change in theological education and ministry.

(2) To take the initiative in pressing the frontier issues of renewal and reform in theological education, and yet to develop a third mandate policy with flexibility and in response to particular local needs and situations as perceived locally. Situations within the Third World do vary; no single directive can meet all needs everywhere. To maintain this stance the TEF must be willing to listen with sensitivity to those voices in the Third World which are defining the shape of responsive faithfulness in theological education in their own areas.

(3) In our consultative and advisory capacities, to be critical of present situations and yet not simply to be critical, some good things are happening; what are they and where, and how can we encourage and support these positive developments? We must be enough committed in a sensitive way to the dominating demand for reform in theological education, and yet modest enough to understand how others in their own situations are defining their problems and seeking solutions appropriate to their culture.

(4) To continue to study and reflect on the issues facing theological education today, and yet not simply become a study team. The process of reflection so prominent during the past two-year study period must be continued, while at the same time the TEF remains precisely a fund with grants to be made in support of undertakings of renewal.

The third mandate's strong emphasis on renewal and reform in theological education appears to focus upon a contral concept, contextuality, the capacity to respond meaningfully to the Gospel within the framework of one's own situation. Contextualization is not simply a fad or catch-word but a theological necessity demanded by the incarnational nature of the Word. What does the term imply?

It means all that is implied in the familiar term "indigenization" and yet seeks to press beyond. Contextualization has to do with how we assess the peculiarity of third
world contexts. Indigenization tends to be used in the
sense of responding to the Gospel in terms of a traditional
culture. Contextualization, while not ignoring this, takes
into account the process of secularity, technology, and the
struggle for human justice, which characterize the historical moment of nations in the Third World.

Yet a careful distinction must be made between authentic
and false forms of contextualization. False contextualization yields to uncritical accommodation, a form of culture
faith. Authentic contextualization is always prophetic,
arising always out of a genuine encounter between God's
Word and His world, and moves toward the purpose of challeng-
ing and changing the situation through rootedness in and
commitment to a given historical moment.

It is therefore clear that contextualization is a dynamic, not a static process. It recognizes the continually
changing nature of every human situation and of the possibility for change, thus opening the way for the future.

The agenda of a Third World contextualizing theology will
have priorities of its own. It may have to express its
self-determination by uninhibitedly opting for a "theology
of change," or by recognizing unmistakable theological significance in such issues as justice, liberation, dialogue with
people of other faiths and ideologies, economic power, etc.

Yet contextualization does not imply the fragmented iso-
lation of peoples and cultures. While within each diverse
cultural situation people must struggle to regain their own
identity and to become subjects of their own history, there
remains an interdependence of contexts. Contextualization
thereby means that the possibilities for renewal must first
of all be sensed locally and situationally, yet always within
the framework of contemporary interdependence which binds
both to the problem of the past and present and to the possibilities for the future.

Finally, contextualization, while it stresses our local
and situational concerns, draws its basic power from the
Gospel, which is for all people. Thus contextualization
contributes ultimately to the solidarity of all people in
obedience to a common Lord.

If, then, contextualization becomes a chief characteristic of authentic theological reflection, a request for support submitted to the TEF will be judged to have potential for renewal when:

(1) There is evidence of contextualization in mission.

(2) There is evidence of contextualization in theological approach.

(3) There is evidence of contextualization in educational method.

(4) There is evidence of contextualization in structure.
(1)

Appendix C
The Theology in the Americas Process

This Process is related to the aftermath of *Theology in the Americas: 1975*, a theological conference held in Detroit in August of that year. The conference brought together Christians from the Americas in an event which had for its starting point the experience of each participant. The aim of Theology in Americas is to "do theology" out of the particular environments of the U.S. experience in order to contribute to the creation of an authentic theology in this country.

I. OBJECTIVES OF THIS PROCESS

A. To develop a new way of doing theology that:

1. grows out of the different social, ethnic, racial and sexual realities

2. incorporates as theological themes, our own histories, the demands and challenges of the Third World, and the structural complexities of this country

3. exemplifies a communal process

B. To explore new methodologies in dealing with the relationship between:

1. truth and practice

2. faith and praxis

3. ideology and faith

C. To confront the dominant theological mainstream with this
   new way of doing theology.

II. THE FRAMEWORK FOR "DOING THEOLOGY"

A. The Meaning of Discipleship

There is a Christian imperative to seek justice and peace.
It is a mandate that requires a radical dealing with the problem of public life, the structure and institutions of society, the policies of governments and political movements
for change.

The mandate given to us by the Lord God is very clear:

> The Spirit of the Lord is upon me; there-
> for he has anointed me. He has sent me
> to bring the good news to the poor, to
> proclaim liberty to the captives, recovery
> of sight to the blind and release to pri-
> soners, to announce a year of favor from
> the Lord. (Luke 4:18-19, Isaiah 61:1)

This mandate is a reflection of the love of God for all people. To be a disciple means to be obedient to this mandate.

God's will and God's love concern all, and the commitment
of Christians in promoting justice is a fundamental response
to Jesus Christ. Liberation is God's intention: liberation
from spiritual, structural and ideological forms of oppression.

There has always been a serious tension between classical
ideas of divine perfection in which God is unaffected by the
sufferings of His people and God as He is revealed in the
Bible as struggling with the rebellions of His people and as
suffering as the result of their disobedience.

The proclamation of the New Testament is the gospel of
the kingdom, a gospel of a "new order," a "new creation," a
"new world," a "new age."

> This means that if anyone is in Christ,
> he is a new creation. The old order has

> passed away; now all is new. All this
> has been done by God, who has reconciled
> us to himself through Christ and has
> given us the ministry of reconciliation.
> (II Corinthians 5:17-18)

To be a disciple of Jesus today in America means not only individual salvation or personal fulfillment. It also means struggle for a new people and a new order.

B. A New People and a New Order

Throughout its history, America has spread hope across the world: its struggle for independence; its call to a democratic way of life; the resistance of its slaves; its abolitionist movement and subsequent Civil War; its feminist movement; and its dramatic labor struggles have all stirred hearts throughout the world.

Perhaps in no other time or place has the struggle for freedom been so dramatic and well known, and yet in the third quarter of the 20th century, many people the world-over perceive America as an enemy of freedom. Why?

For many people of the U.S., the horrors of Vietnam, Watergate, the CIA interventions in Chile and elsewhere, the vulnerability of our government officials to bribery and corruption, etc. have forced us to re-evaluate our history as a people in light of our present situation as a nation. For some, there is a growing awareness that in a certain sense there are two Americas; namely, the America of its ordinary people and the America of a small but powerful group who dominate and control the nation.

In this perspective, when voices of protest arise in the world against America, they are not condemning the American people as such; rather they are cries of protest against the transnational elites whose international structural control is founded on the exploitation of people both in this country and in other areas of the world.

Theology in the Americas invites people to understand better the American reality and to deepen the analysis of the causes of our problems. It especially wants to explore one aspect of the reality in which Americans live: the dynamics of power and powerlessness in the present American experience.

To understand the meaning of Christian faith, the Christian community must come to a correct understanding of its concrete historical situation. Conversion to God implies self-knowledge. This principle should be taken up by local Christian communities as they struggle for a correct collective understanding of their concrete historical task of the present moment.

A New People and a New Order are the two aims of Theology in the Americas. Formation of a new people means repentance and conversion; formation of a new order means working for new societal structures. Both personal conversion and structural reform are essential ingredients in the Theology in the Americas process.

C. The Collective Process

The emphasis is on the experience and reflection of groups more than that of individuals. This style of critical reflection tries to replace the highly competitive understanding that makes room for contributions from various perspectives.

The individualistic context of research and reflection is completed and enlarged with the communal process of entry into truth.

The process is primarily for believers, that is, for people of faith, involving the re-interpretation of Christian symbols and the transformation of structures in the churches as well as in society.

Jesus and the churches are present and alive in this process. On one side, people are believers trying to be obedient to the Lord Jesus Christ; on the other side, they want to uncover how the dominant Christian theologies reflect the life experiences and interests of the privileged sectors of society and serve to perpetuate the status quo.

III.   CRITERIA FOR PARTICIPATION IN THIS PROCESS

A. Reflection which Starts from Praxis

There are two meanings of the word "praxis" that will be important for our emphasis here: One is the different way of knowing truth; the other is the relationship between praxis and theology.

1. *A different way of knowing the truth*. The traditional
way of knowing considers the truth as the conformity of the
mind to a given object. This way is part of the Greek influence in the Western philosophical tradition. Such a concept of truth only conforms to and legitimatizes the world
as it now exists.

But there is another way of knowing the truth--a dialectical one. In this case, the world is not a static object
which the human mind confronts and attempts to understand;
rather, the world is an unfinished project which is being
built. Knowledge is not the conformity of the mind to the
given, but an immersion in this process of transformation
and construction of a new world.

This new epistemology (way of knowing) has to be applied
to the "revealed truth of Christianity." The theological
truth is not only the conformity of the mind to revelation
as it is contained in Scripture; it is also the discernment
of present evil in the world and in hearts, judged by the
message of the gospel and the discovery of the movement of
redemptive and liberating history. Divine truth is redemptive, but the norm of theological truth comes from its role
in the ongoing process of world-building.

2. *Praxis--Faith--Theological Reflection*. The starting
point of theology is faith. But faith not just as an intel-
lectual concept or acceptance of the message of the gospel,
but as an encounter with the Lord, as love and commitment to
others. To have faith means to follow Jesus, to be obedient
to the authority of the Word of God by making it alive in
serving our sisters and brothers.

Social analysis interprets love and translates commitment
into a context of practice or praxis. Personal praxis is
the participation in the process of transformation of society.
God is leading the world toward the "new heaven and the new
earth." Through praxis, people enter into their historical
destiny. Praxis means action combined with theory; action
shapes theory which then redirects action, and so on--all
situated within a global perspective. As people engage in
praxis, both they and their world change.

Therefore, praxis becomes the starting point for a clearer
vision of the action of God in history. It is necessary,
therefore, to relate Christian theory with historical move-
ment--to interlock faith with praxis. Interpreted in the
light of Christian faith, praxis acquires a deep meaning,

for it is perceived as the locus where the Promise of the salvation of Jesus is fulfilled and where Christian faith and fidelity are verified.

B. Consideration of Particularities--Emphasis on Affinity Groups

In doing theology, we must be aware of the ways in which our understanding is conditioned by our social context. The social sciences help to uncover how each person's consciousness is influenced from birth by the experiences of the family, by the larger social group within which the family exists, and by the social structures within which social groups exist and relate to one another. As members of social groups, our theology is significantly conditioned.

Black theology offers a powerful example of sensitivity to the distortions of a racist society. Similar examples of this kind of sensitivity to social context can be found in theology being done in communities of different racial and ethnic origins. Feminists provide still another example of seeing through the historical sexist fabric of society. Class differences too are central in our society, for we live in hierarchical structures which keep us from sensing our oneness as a people. These conflicts are reproduced throughout the world in the violent struggles between rich countries and poor countries.

Because of the important particularities to be explored by people who suffer the consequences of racist, ethnic, sexist, and/or classist oppression, it is difficult at this moment to speak of one North American Theology. The primary emphasis at this time is on the common action/reflection of Affinity Groups. Nevertheless, at the same time we must also stress our united struggle, and continue to enrich and challenge each other by sharing the insights each Affinity Group perceives from its own particular experience.

C. Social Analysis and Theology

1. *Social Analysis*. Today, Theology has to use sociology and psychology to explain the world. But it is not clear how the social sciences are an integral part of theology as are philosophy and other traditional disciplines. Besides that, it is necessary to demystify the so-called "value-neutral" analysis of social sciences as they interpret the U.S. reality "empirically." A model for analysis is needed that will help to understand better the society in which we live.

There is no room for dogmatism here, but only for scientific research based on the actual historical situation confronting us. Durkeim, Max Weber, and Marx, among others, have made significant contributions to analysis in this respect.

It will behoove us to be open to the appropriation of socio-political analysis to theology and faith as we struggle to seek out the will of God for the U.S. in this historical moment. Indeed, without doing so, it will be difficult for us to respond authentically to the challenge Jesus offers us in the parable of the Good Samaritan to "go and do the same" (Luke 10:37).

2. *From Particular Experience to a Global Vision.* One of the main problems of many Christian groups in the U.S. is that they are involved in concrete issues and struggles concerning housing, food, health care, reform of prison systems, deterioration of neighborhoods, etc., but they lack an analysis that will enable them to situate these absolutely necessary struggles within a global framework. What is needed is an analysis that will help them to see the connection between local issues and global realities, between national problems and international structures.

It will be crucial to interpret critically our own national history and to discover the positive as well as the negative elements within our traditions that can be called upon to foster holistic change. Systemic global analysis can promote the emergence of alternative visions of what the U.S.A. can be, in response to oppressed groups' struggles for liberation both here and abroad.

D. International Responsibility

The U.S.A. is the leader of one part of the world. Even if its leadership has been challenged in recent years by the countries of the Third World, it remains in control of a disproportionate share of power, technology, food, and influence.

It is now widely recognized that there is a basic conflict going on in the world between the rich and the poor countries: one side seeks to maintain the present world economic system while the other side demands a new economic order more equitable for the total global population. To reflect theologically on the American experience cannot be separated from the inter-relatedness of this experience to the international scene. Indeed, it is an essential responsibility of Christian people.

E. The Theological Dimension

Even though the conditions listed here are all elements
of the process for theological reflection in a new perspective, it is necessary to deal with theologizing more specifically.

Our religious tradition demands that we ask how God is
present today in the midst of social structures which promote exploitation and oppression. God's revelation in the
Exodus event and in the scandal of Jesus' mission among the
oppressed points to a demand for involvement in the situation of the poor.

Our theological reflection is related to praxis, but
praxis cannot be reduced to theology, nor theology to praxis.
But theology is done *in the process* of praxis—one moment
toward the global transformation of society toward a new
vision.

Religious tradition reveals a God in history speaking
through the struggles of the poor and the oppressed. Scripture calls us to focus our understanding of God's Word
through participation with the oppressed in struggles for
liberation.

F. The Challenge of Commitment

1. *Openness to Political Commitment.* There is a traditional mistrust of political activity among Christians. Both
historical and doctrinal reasons support this attitude, but
can a Christian today still confess commitment to Jesus and
not be involved politically?

In the process we have described above, the political implications of Christianity are very demanding. Either we re-
main unconscious of the conflict and violence taking place
at the heart of our society and fall back upon individualistic theological perspectives, and thus support the *status
quo*, or we come to grips with the structural dimensions of
oppression and opt for change.

Coalitions for social change at different levels are good,
but they are not enough. Until political power is used for
human liberation—until the power of the U.S.A. serves the
cause of the poor within its own borders and the poor countries in the world—there can be no rest for American Christians.

2. *Evangelical Life Style.*   Social change is needed and
reform of structures is indispensable.   But this is only one
side of commitment.   The other side is conversion, repentance, "metanoia" of the individual person.   Both political
and lifestyle options form a true evangelical response to the
Lord Jesus, as we try to live the gospel in both our personal
lives and in confronting the evils in societal structures.

"From that time on, Jesus began to preach and to say:
'Repent, for the Kingdom of God is at hand'" (Matthew 4:17).
At the outset of His ministry, Jesus proclaims the coming of
the Kingdom and calls women and men to a complete change of
heart and mind.   He says that entering the Kingdom comes
through repentance and radical transformation.   We interpret
this call as applicable not only to our personal lives but
to transforming the oppressive structures of our society as
well.

IV.   THE PROCESS OF DOING THEOLOGY

Traditionally, theology has been linked with the life of
the Church.   To do theology in the "context" of society
means that theology has to interpret and critically analyze
the salvific action of God in the social and political efforts taking place for social change and liberation. While it
is difficult to separate methodology and content in theology,
it is helpful to consider them in a different perspective.

A. Hermeneutics and Content of Theology

In doing theology, it is necessary to be aware of the
ways in which the understanding of scripture is conditioned
by the social context in which it is considered.   Just as
the social sciences have not been value-free, so too we find
that Biblical interpretation has been conditioned by Greek
philosophical categories.   Also we encounter a cultural cap-
tivity in the western individualistic and affluent perspective that theologians have used previously that is necessary
to unmask.   Until now, few theologians have questioned the
values and structures of the economic and social systems
that support oppression and imperialism.

Some Christians are aware that scriptural exegesis and
Church doctrine cannot be considered as something suspended
above the level of social conditioning: it too reflects the
prejudices, values and conflicts of this historical moment.
Therefore, theology does not come through an unsullied pipe-
line connecting scripture to contemporary times.

A theological method is needed that does justice to the authority of scripture and to the present experiences of the people of God so that there is an authentic participation in the liberating action of God. It is necessary to uncover the role of ideology in the study of the scriptures and theological reflection, always trying to respond to the will of God as revealed both in scripture and in the "signs of the times."

B. Possible Theological Themes

As we have seen, it is urgent to have a correct understanding of the will of God to guide our present struggles and chart the future. God is calling American Christians to conversion, and our obedience to the Lord Jesus urges us to speak of him from the midst of on-going crisis of institutions and of hearts.

In this light, it is necessary to explore some theological themes that need to be re-examined with the insights gained through praxis. Such themes might be included in the agenda for Theology in the Americas:

-- the intrinsic relations between sin and salvation on the one hand, and the historical process and struggle for socio-political liberation on the other.

-- the continuing presence and action of God in our history and the response this elicits by believing Christians.

-- the relation between the new and old world constructs; the relationship between this world and the other world.

-- the discontinuity between the Kingdom Christ envisioned and the historical process in which the Church is involved.

CONCLUSION

Thus we see that the Theology in the Americas process is both a search for a new way of being Christian, confronted with the systemic sin of our times, and a renouncing of a more comfortable, but surely less life-giving way of professing faith in the gospel. Theology in the Americas is an invitation to Christians to begin to look for new ways of being

Christians in a very complex national situation that bears
international dimensions. The task before us is a momentous
one, but one we must respond to if we heed seriously the
call to "make all things new" in Christ Jesus.

                              The Secretariat
                              Theology in the Americas
                              December, 1976

Appendix D
Contextualization
of North American Theology

INTRODUCTION

This Program is related to the follow-up of "THEOLOGY IN THE AMERICAS: 1975," a theological conference held in Detroit in August 1975. That conference brought together Christians from the Americas in an event which had for a starting point the experience of each participant. The conference, like the preparation process, had a modest goal, a tentative probing. The intent was not to create a new U.S. theology, or to translate Latin American theology, but simply to explore new possibilities of theological methodology and reflection.

Detroit was a Christian event of people of faith. All of them agreed that theology is the acceptance of the Divine Revelation in Jesus Christ. The common ground was the biblical faith: "God so loved the world that He gave His only Son, that whoever believes in Him may not die, but may have eternal life" (John 3:16-18).

But there was a difference in the understanding of theology. People in Detroit understood that the Word of God is not only present in the experience of Israel and in the Person of Jesus Christ, as recorded in Scripture and preached by the Church, but the Word of God is also present in a more hidden and provisional way in the whole of human life.

The task of theology, understood in this perspective, is to detect the forces of destruction and the powers of healing, both of which are at work in the world. These powers

of destruction and healing are the "context" of the Word and
the action of God in history. For this very reason it is
necessary to talk about the Contextualization of North American Theology.

I.   CONTEXTUALIZATION OF NORTH AMERICAN THEOLOGY

The future of North American theology concerns many people today, especially those who are preoccupied with the
concepts of pluralism and the contextualization of theology.
We hear about Latin American, African and Asian theologies.
What we call Western theology has been largely, if not exclusively, a European theology.

This seems for many Christians the right time to develop
more authentic North American theologies. Otherwise, Christianity in the United States will lack the prophetic voice
required of it by the ecumenical demands of today and the
future.

The context would include many different aspects and issues, one of which, by itself, is far-reaching. The U.S.
dominates a large part of the world in economic and technological power. There must be a critical Christian word addressed to the great human issues that arise just from that
fact.

The American dream has been increasingly challenged in
the last years. For many North Americans, U.S. history expressed in religious symbols is a covenant of freedom and
democracy. For some people at home and many in the Third
World, it is an enterprise of oppression, domination and
imperialism.

North American theology has to be concerned with the
deeper questions of how to speak of Christ in the midst of
the ongoing moral crisis of the U.S. It is necessary to
recover the tradition of idealism and struggle against oppression in our own history, both secular and religious, and
work toward shaping a theology for the future.

There are many perspectives for such a task. Since theology is not the Word of God itself, but a reflection on that
Word from the present perspective, the question of the future of theology has to deal with all the claims of Christ
over contemporary realities. Politics, language, mass media,
education, ecology, urbanization, behavioral sciences, and
technology affect the language and mission of the Christian
communities.

This Program seeks to explore one aspect of the "context" of the reality in which Americans live: the dynamics of power and powerlessness in the present American experience. The Christian community must first understand its concrete historical situation. Conversion to God implies self-knowledge. This principle also applies to communities; they must come to a collective self-understanding that corresponds to their historical situation.

The political experience of the U.S. involves two levels: the international responsibility and the domestic complexity and variety of forms of domination and oppression. A North American theology will be different from European theology or Latin American theology. But it is urgent for Christians in the U.S. to have a deep understanding of the will of God for our present and our future. God is calling American Christians to conversion, and our obedience to the Lord demands a critical evaluation of the uses and abuses of U.S. power.

II.   THE BIBLE AS THE NORM OF THEOLOGY

All Christians acknowledge the Scriptures as the norm of the Church's faith and practice. We agree that in Israel and in Jesus Christ, God has made himself manifest in a definitive and unconditional way and we hold that the written record of this Sacred History gives the Church access to these divine events as the source of her wisdom.

We read in the Epistle to the Hebrews: "In times past, God spoke in fragmentary and varied ways to our forbears through the prophets; in this, the final stage, he has spoken to us through his Son. . ."(Hebrews 1:1-2).

But when theologians try to determine the meaning and message of Jesus Christ and apply the Scriptures as the measure of the Church's life, they often disagree.

At one time the disagreement on the normative function of the Bible defined the confessional differences between Catholics and Protestants. Today it seems that the disagreements cut across these ecclesiastical boundaries.

Theology in the Americas believes that the old ecclesiastical and doctrinal disputes that have divided the Church for so long are not relevant anymore. There is a change in the focus of theology and a change in the methodology of theology. In the past, the questions in traditional theology

were raised from within the ecclesiastical institutions.
Today, while not abandoning that perspective, Christians and
theologians want to understand the meaning of the Word of
God present as judgment and grace in history, both personal
and social--of this generation.

This Program attempts to explore new theological methods.
The experience of the work in Detroit indicates three(3):

A. The Experience of Ordinary Christians

Theologizing no longer means simply studying sources and
ideas in the seminaries or universities. That is not enough.
Theology has to spring from the experiences of all Christians, both academicians and non-academicians, who are trying to discover Christ in the Scriptures and in their own
lives. There will be a special effort to relate to the experience of oppressed people who are struggling for their
liberation here in this country and abroad.

Liberation is God's intention: liberation from spiritual,
structural and ideological forms of oppression:

> The Spirit of the Lord is upon me; there-
> for he has anointed me.
> He has sent me to bring the good news to
> the poor, to proclaim liberty to the cap-
> tives, recovery of sight to the blind and
> release to prisoners, to announce a year
> of favor from the Lord. (Luke 4:18-19;
> Isaiah 61:1)

This North American theology will be done, primarily,
though not exclusively, by groups of the oppressed themselves and will arise out of their own particular experience
of oppression. The assessment of the evil powers which oppress people in their concrete situation is an essential
part of theology, for without it the meaning of divine revelation cannot be grasped.

B. Theology and Social Sciences

It is clear for theologians today that theology has to
use sociology and psychology to explain the world. But it
is not clear how the social sciences are an integral part of
theology as are philosophy and other traditional disciplines.
Besides that, it is necessary to demystify the so-called
value-neutral analysis of social scientists who interpret the
U.S. reality.

The task of developing a structural analysis of the U.S.
is increasingly seen as integral to theological reflection,
suggesting a promising new methodology in North American
theology.

C. Theory and Practice

There has been a change in the understanding of truth, in
the sociology of knowledge in general and in theology in
particular. Thinking is not now considered prior or super-
ior to action, rather, it takes place in action. The Christian religion was founded not on a word, but on the Word
made Flesh. Faith is no longer simply "applied" or "completed" in action, but for its very understanding (and this
is theology) faith demands that it be discovered in action.

It is necessary to relate Christian theory and historical
praxis, faith and practice. Some theologians are talking of
a theology defined as critical reflection on the historical
praxis. Practice refers to any action that applies a particular theory. Praxis is practice associated with a total
dynamics of historical vision and social transformation.
Through praxis, people enter into their historical destiny.
Since praxis changes the world as well as the actors it becomes the starting point for a clearer vision of God in history.

This way of conceiving the truth finds an explicit con-
firmation in the Johannine emphasis on "doing the truth."
God's Word--His Logos--is an Incarnate Word, human flesh
which has pitched its tent in history. Knowledge of such
Logos is fellowship, participation in this new life which
has been made available in the midst of the old world. It
is a "new birth" (John 3:3). There is no way of understanding the new teaching through mere exegetical exercise. "Why
do you not understand what I say? It is because you cannot
bear to hear my word" (John 8:43).

One must be ready to enter actively into this relation,
this life: only the person who *does* the word will know the
doctrine.

This Program will explore this new way of knowing and its
implications for theological reflection. Instead of talking
about studying theology it seems better to begin "doing theology"--that is, to discover the meaning of Revelation in the
midst of experience and the struggle for change and conversion.

III. THE OBJECTIVES OF THIS PROGRAM

In light of the above, three specific objectives have evolved for the Theology in the Americas:

A. To develop a new way of doing theology that:

1. grows out of the different social, ethnic, racial and sexual realities

2. incorporates as theological themes, our own histories, the demands and challenges of the Third World, and the structural complexities of this country

3. exemplifies a communal process

B. To explore new methodologies in dealing with the relationship between:

1. truth and practice

2. faith and praxis

3. ideology and faith

C. To confront the dominant theological mainstream with this new way of doing theology.

IV. THE CONSTITUENCIES, STRUCTURES AND ORGANIZATION

The Conference in Detroit was conceived as one moment in an ongoing process of action and reflection which begin about a year prior to the week in Detroit and would continue in a deepened and expanded form.

For some months prior to the conference about sixty "reflection groups" around the country prepared for it. To some extent the conference program and format were a product of the combined reflection and analysis of many different groups.

This continues to be the model of action and reflection for the follow up. People who attended Detroit and others who did not attend but who are interested will continue this program of action, reflection, study and prayer. Theologians, Christian social activists, directors of theological education, social scientists and racial/ethnic minorities who accept the criteria for participation will be part of this new theological endeavor.

The Executive Committee

The Executive Committee is the group that is responsible for the program. It is composed of representatives of Affinity Groups determined in Detroit, Church leaders and workers, and theologians.

V. THE PROJECTS

To implement the objectives of Theology in the Americas, a series of projects has been developed. These projects bring together representatives of the different Affinity Groups to deepen their theological understanding in the context of the whole North American society.

Project 1. Task Force of Professional Theologians

White U.S. Professional theologians have been the focus of much criticism. As representatives of the dominant culture and theological establishment they have a special role in the evaluation and reformulation of an indigenous theological methodology and content.

Tasks of this group:

1. To incorporate into our theological reflection explicit awareness of the ways in which different forms of oppression, like racism, sexism, class exploitation and imperialism, are interstructured and mutually reinforcing on a world scale.

2. To develop a resource pool of theologians and theological materials which can be made available to reflection groups in their ongoing efforts to do theology.

3. To help articulate, in response to Christian revelation and the cries of the oppressed, a vision of a better world.

4. To critically examine theological education and its role in the churches and in the larger society.

Project 2. Women's Project

Out of their experience of becoming aware of sexism as a
distinct form of oppression, historically interrelated with
economic and racial oppression, women have already begun to
make a major contribution to the reshaping of theology in
the industrialized world. The conclusion in Detroit was
that unless those who struggle against economic exploitation
and racial injustice become conscious of their ancient sexist heritage, they will not significantly alter the situation of women.

Aim. This project will deepen and expand women's theological explorations by adding to the feminist dynamic the
critique of race, class and imperialism. Out of this project will come a greater clarity about the nature and func-
tioning of sexism for perpetuating systems of injustice and
a new solidarity among women in the struggles against various forms of oppression. Hopefully, too, this will impact
the consciousness of men.

Implementation. Groups of white, middle-class women,
women of different ethnic and class backgrounds will engage
in action/reflection on the interstructuring of racism, sexism, and class exploitation, especially as they impact women
--such action/reflection is seen as integral to the theological process. Resources will be shared, networks established
and regionally-based ways found for women of varying backgrounds to coalesce around issues of mutual concern.

Project 3. Black Theology Project

There will be a theological Consultation in the Interdenominational Theological Consortium (ITC) in Atlanta,
Georgia in August, 1977.

Aim. To bring together Black representatives of religious and secular institutions to discuss theologically the
theme, National and International Priorities of Black Theology, as they relate to the Black Church and the Black Community.

Participants. Black theologians, scholars of religious
studies, ministers of different churches, social scientists,
Christian social activists, community organizers, and grass
roots Blacks.

Preparation. The preparation for the Conference has already started. It will be a process similar to that which was developed prior to the Detroit Conference. Action/reflection groups will be established in areas with a large Black population. These groups will study and discuss the different aspects of the theme of the Conference.

Sponsors. Black seminaries, departments dealing with the Blacks in the Denominations, community organizations, etc.

Project 4. Hispanic Consultation

Aim. To develop a religious interpretation of the relations among the Hispanic groups, the established churches and the dominant culture of the U.S.

Implementation. A series of forums, dialogues, seminars will be established in various structured and unstructured formats. A theological consultation will be held in Texas in August of 1978. The theme will be "Hispanic-American Theology in the North American Context."

Participants. Mexican-Americans, Puerto Ricans and other Hispanic-American groups will be invited to reflect on their religious and cultural heritage as well as on their dialectical relationships with the U.S. society.

Organization. The participants and sponsors are presently being considered by Hispanic-American representatives. They are contacting heads of Hispanic departments in the denominations, dioceses and seminaries, as well as ministers and leaders of community organizations, etc. in Hispanic communities.

Project 5. Labor and Church Dialogue

Aim. To channel the anxieties and struggles of the U.S. workers toward a common analysis and response to their situation in light of the international struggle of workers throughout the world, and also in the light of the Christian principles of social justice; concurrently, to sensitize the churches to the reality of the plight of the U.S. working class.

Implementation. This project will attempt to simultaneously: 1) develop a network of individuals and groups within the churches interested and involved in questions of Labor Movements and 2) conduct a series of workshops with

workers for a clearer definition of their issues. After
these first explorations, there can be published some tentative conclusions regarding working class aspirations, frus-
trations, living conditions, expectations from their churches,
etc. From these conclusions, a viable action plan could
be developed.

Project 6. The White Theology Project

The Project of the White Affinity Group is composed of
three separate and interrelated units: reflection, dialogue
and education. The first of these units involves a collective reflection within the White Affinity Group itself.
This group may be described as white Christians working toward justice who share the assumptions of Theology in the
Americas. The second unit is one of outreach and education
among white Christians who are concerned with finding ways
of understanding and acting out the biblical mandate to love
one another in a society that experiences many structural
barriers to effective love. The third unit is one of dialogue with Christian evangelicals who are exploring and acting on concerns similar to those of the White Affinity Group.

Each unit will require a different set of organizational
structures. Yet, together, the units comprise an effort to
deepen our understanding of the theological task by more
precisely enabling the doing of theology. This task is
undertaken in the context of the experience and work of each
group involved.

Project 7. Asian Americans in the U.S. Context

Asian Americans presently represent the most rapidly growing immigrant group in the U.S., when considering percentages.
An indigenous group has been developing a national organization with regional groups. Programs for theological reflection and building strategies are conducted for clergy and
laity. Resource materials are produced and circulated. Concrete action is taken to mitigate the racism in churches,
educational institutions, and selected community issues.

Aim. The indigenous organization (PACTS, Pacific and
Asian Center for Theology and Strategies) would seek to relate the emerging structures, processes, and actions to
other groups in the program of Contextualization of North
American Theology.

Implementation. The decisions affecting Asian Americans would be determined by the indigenous group, as it seeks to coordinate its work with other groups.

Project 8. Land, Native Americans and Red Theology

Since the discovery of the Americas in 1492, the native people of both North and South America have resisted the colonialism of white European cultures. However, after the establishment of the United States, colonialism continued and focused primarily on the lands occupied by the numerous Indian nations.

The issues of current importance to the Indian movement today are mostly the ancient, unresolved constitutional issues and rights arising from treaties. Beyond this, all the social, economic and cultural problems of an oppressed minority are present on the reservations and in the urban areas where Native Americans live.

Aims. 1) To contact the organization of Native Americans at the grass roots levels. 2) To evaluate the action of the churches in their efforts of "Evangelization" of the Native Americans. 3) To encourage the development of a process of theological reflection from the experience of oppression of the Native Americans. 4) To relate the beginning of a Red Theology to developments in Black, Hispanic, White, Feminist and other forms of theologizing from the perspective of oppression.

VI. THE INTERNATIONAL DIMENSION

People engaged in the Theology in the Americas action/ reflection process do not look exclusively at the various kinds of oppression that effects them in their personal situation nor do they focus solely on the oppressive structures existing within the borders of the United States. It is essential to link both of these to an analysis of the global situation of structural injustice and exploitation of peoples by groups and institutions more powerful than themselves.

Because this international dimension is integral to the objectives of Theology in the Americas and yet goes beyond the immediate scope of the program, a similar program intrinsically related to Theology in the Americas exists. This program, Ecumenical Dialogue of Third World Theologians, facilitates an ongoing exchange between theologians, church leaders, and grassroots Christians of Africa, Asia, and Latin America who attempt to deepen their understanding of what God's will is for their people today.

Just as Theology in the Americas' goal is to develop an authentic North American Theology born out of the struggles of its people, so too, Ecumenical Dialogue of Third World Theologians attempts to contextualize theologically the struggles for liberation of Third World peoples.

VII. THE FIVE-YEAR PLAN

This program is a response to the felt needs to give priority to a theology that emerges from the experiences of Christians and that reflects upon the social, political, economic and cultural situation in the USA. It is not intended to be a theological center or a permanent organization.

In brief, the five-year plan is as follows:

1975	- "Theology in the Americas" Conference in Detroit
1976-1979	- Initiation and development of Projects, as follow-up of the Detroit Conference
1980	- "The Contextualization of US Theology," a consultation similar to the Detroit Conference, which will include an evaluation of the five years and projections for the future.

VIII. PARTICIPATION AND SUPPORT

This proposal is being presented to people and institutions interested in the future of Christianity in this country and in the future of the missionary enterprise in the world.

Participation is meant to deepen a new theological vision for people working in three main areas:

1. *National Ministries*. Grass roots involved in Christian social action: religious and lay personnel of local congregations; heads of commissions dealing with ministries in the U.S.

2. *Overseas Ministries*. Missionaries serving in other continents; heads of missions dealing with overseas ministries.

3. *Theological Community*. Professional theologians and directors of theological education in the denominations as well as in seminaries and universities.

There are many programs presented to these groups and institutions. This program is not intended to duplicate what other groups and commissions are already doing; rather it attempts to work in collaboration with other efforts while maintaining the originality and uniqueness of its approach and method of theological research.

IX. CONCRETE ACTION

The concrete actions asked of persons and institutions interested in this proposal are the following:

1. Involvement in different levels of the program through people working in areas similar to the Projects specified above.

2. Financial contribution toward the budget for the program.

3. Offering of in-kind support, e.g., office facilities, secretarial aid, etc.

Notes

CHAPTER 1

[1]Shoki Coe, "Authentic contextuality leads to contextualization,"
Theological Education 9 (Summer 1973):24-25.

[2]J. K. Agbeti, "African Theology: What It Is," *Presence* 5
(1972):6.

[3]Charles R. Taber, "What is Mission All About?" *Milligan Missio-
gram* 1 (Spring 1974):4.

[4]John 14:26.

[5]Matthew 28:19-20.

[6]Interview with Lucy K. of Nairobi area, Indiana, Penn., January
1977.

[7]John L. Nevius, *Planting and Development of Missionary Churches*,
4th ed. (Philadelphia: Presbyterian & Reformed Publishing Co., 1958).
This book was developed from articles first published in 1885. Roy
E. Shearer describes the Nevius Method as "1. Self-support required
the Korean Christians to build their own churches and pay their own
pastors. 2. Self-government early placed the Korean Christians in
charge of their own affairs. 3. Self-propagation stressed the responsibility of each Christian to win those around him to Christ."
Roy E. Shearer, *Wildfire: Church Growth in Korea* (Grand Rapids:
Wm. B. Eerdmans Pub. Co., 1966), p. 238.

[8]Kosuke Koyama, *Waterbuffalo Theology* (Maryknoll, N.Y.: Orbis
Books, 1974), pp. 78-88.

[9]E. Bolaji Idowu, *Towards an Indigenous Church* (Ibadan: Oxford
University Press, 1965), p. 37.

[10]Hereafter referred to as evangelicals.

[11]The evangelical hermeneutic will be discussed in the presentation of Chapter IV below, pp. 78-88. This writer is well aware of the difficulty of making such distinctions as the threefold division above. On the issue of contextualization of theology, however, such a grouping will aid in analysis of the situation.

[12]Donald A. McGavran, *The Clash Between Christianity and Cultures* (Washington, D.C.: Canon Press, 1974), pp. 1-10.

[13]Leonard T. Wolcott, "In Defense of Missions," *Christianity Today*, 16 January 1976, pp. 15-17.

[14]Theological Education Fund, *Ministry in Context* (Bromley, Kent, United Kingdom: New Life Press, 1972). TEF is sponsored by the Commission on World Mission and Evangelism of the Faith and Witness program unit of the World Council of Churches. It was formed in 1958.

[15]Ibid., pp. 18-19.

[16]The first mandate involved raising the level of scholarship and striving for academic excellence in theological training in the Third World. The second mandate shifted the emphasis to missionary orientation and thrust, and to training which was intended to lead to a real encounter between the student and the gospel in terms of his own forms of thought and culture. See Harvie M. Conn, "Theological Reflections on Contextualizing Christianity: How Far Do We Go?" paper presented at the joint NAE-EFMA meeting, Arlington Heights, Ill., Spring 1977, p. 1.

[17]TEF, *Ministry in Context*, p. 15.

[18]Ibid., p. 88.

[19]At this point Nissiotis was most likely coloring the **contextualization discussion by his Eastern Orthodox presuppositions.** Others proved to be more radical. Nissiotis' letter in Notes from the Bossey folder. Personal files of John F. Robinson. Photocopies in this writer's possession.

[20]Bishop Festo Kivengere commented on the relevancy of the Christian message. "The Gospel is not relevant. It is indispensable. You just don't preach it because it fits into a situation. You preach it because it's indispensable." From address to the School of World Mission and Evangelism Colloquium, Trinity Evangelical Divinity School, January, 1976.

[21]"The contextual tendency works more with theological fragments, analyzing particular themes and situations which arrest attention." A. O. Dyson, "Dogmatic or Contextual Theology?" *Study Encounter* 8 (1972):2.

[22]A colorful list of fragments has evolved. They are called at times, "theologies of. . ." The list includes a theology of rainmaking, a theology of child raising, and even a theology of roadbuilding.

[23]Robinson, notes.

[24]This belief was one of the main affirmations of the Commission on World Mission and Evangelism of the WCC at the Mexico, 1963 meeting. See summary by A. P. Johnston, "Joint Action in Mission, Mexico, 1963," a paper presented at Trinity Evangelical Divinity School, Deerfield, Ill., 5 November 1976 (typewritten), p. 3.

[25]Robinson, notes. See discussion on this theological position below, pp. 14-19.

[26]Robinson, notes.

[27]"The crisis" is referred to several times in the various TEF documents and discussion. See TEF, *Ministry in Context*, p. 88, for one example.

[28]Dyson, "Theology?" p. 8.

[29]Robinson, notes. See extended quote above, pp. 5-6.

[30]Dyson, "Theology?" p. 8. He reflects much of the theological biases of the early 70s. For more on that era see below on the history of theology in the 60s, pp. 13-32.

[31]Ibid., p. 6.

[32]Dyson, "Theology?" p. 4.

[33]Ibid., p. 6.

[34]Burns' suggestion recorded in Rev. Gerald Krohn notes, taken at the Ecumenical Institute, Bossey, Switzerland, 1959.

[35]Ibid.

[36]A. O. Dyson, "Theology?" p. 5.

[37]Because of the close affinity of the methodology and contents of political theology with contextualized theology, a discussion of the development and some of the major themes of political theology are included in Chapter II below, pp. 13-32.

[38]One has to commend those who stress the action of God in the now. Those who perceive God's interaction with man, moment by moment, are truly aware of the One who is above us yet with us (Joshua 1:9). But this emphasis on dynamic relationships should not be allowed to reduce the importance of the propositional truths of the Scriptures or the distinct Person behind those truths. Much emphasis on dynamics at the expense of a personal interaction with objective truth appears to be a type of "doublethink" with the shift being from the language of metaphysics to physics. Harold O. J. Brown commented on the process:

> Most recently, however, there has been a tendency
> to say not that the orthodox Christology is false
> but that it is inappropriate. One should not ask
> what Christ is (God and Man), but what He *does*
> (saves us). This rather glib dismissal of convic-
> tions for which early Christians suffered and died
> as not untrue but *irrelevant* is justified by re-
> ference to the fact that it involves a *dynamic*
> rather than a static understanding of Christ. The
> rhetorical importation of the terminology of phy-
> sics should not obscure the essential truth that
> Jesus the Messiah could do what He did only because
> He is who and what He is: the only Begotten of the
> Father, very God and very Man.

Harold O. J. Brown, "The Conservative Option," *Tensions in Contemporary Theology*, eds. Stanley N. Gundry and Alan F. Johnson (Chicago:
Moody Press, 1976), p. 355.

[39] Robinson, notes, p. 3.

CHAPTER 2

[1] To be considered in Chapter 3 below, pp. 33-51.

[2] Alistair Kee, ed., *A Reader in Political Theology* (Philadelphia:
Westminster Press, 1974).

[3] For an introductory discussion on process theology from the
viewpoint of a conservative evangelical (and Thomist) see Norman L.
Geisler, "Process Theology," in *Tensions in Contemporary Theology*,
eds. Stanley N. Gundry and Alan F. Johnson, pp. 235-284.

[4] David F. Wells, "Recent Roman Catholic Theology," in *Tensions
in Contemporary Theology*, eds. Stanley N. Gundry and Alan F. Johnson,
pp. 287-324; also David F. Wells, *Revolution in Rome* Downers Grove,
Ill.: Inter-Varsity Press, 1972), pp. 121-123.

[5] Margaret Montagno, Peter Younghusband, and Pamela Abramson, "The
Missionary's Lot," *Newsweek*, 4 April 1977, p. 90.

[6] Liberation theology was given very significant impetus at the
Bishops' Conference at Medellin in 1968. The philosophies of Marx
and Bloch and the theologies of Moltmann and Metz were integral to
the thought, supplementing the results of Vatican II theology.

[7] Jurgen Moltmann, *Theology of Hope* (Evanston: Harper & Row, 1967),
p. 21.

[8] Kee, *Reader*, pp. 2-3.

[9] David Scaer, "Theology of Hope," in *Tensions in Contemporary
Theology*, eds. Stanley N. Gundry and Alan F. Johnson, p. 210.

[10] Moltmann, *Theology of Hope*, p. 16.

[11]Christopher Larson, "Theology of Hope: a Review," *Trinity Studies* 2 (1972):103.

[12]Moltmann, *Theology of Hope*, p. 16.

[13]Ibid., pp. 24, 301, 305.

[14]Ibid., p. 323. Jose Miguez-Bonino makes a critique similar to Moltmann's.

> Why is it, for instance, that the obvious political motifs and undertones in the life of Jesus have remained so hidden to liberal interpreters until very recently? Is this merely a regrettable oversight on the part of these scholars or is it—mostly unconscious, to be sure—the expression of the liberal **ideological** distinction of levels or spheres which relegates religion to the area of subjectivity and individual privacy?

Jose Miguez-Bonino, *Doing Theology in a Revolutionary Situation* (Philadelphia: Fortress Press, 1975), p. 91.

[15]Moltmann, *Theology of Hope*, p. 260.

[16]Ibid., p. 261.

[17]Ibid., p. 289.

[18]Ibid., p. 288. When Moltmann rejected the Greek view of history and God as unmoved mover, he seems also to have rejected the Lord of the Scriptures, who is Creator and Providential Lord of history. As Christopher Larson observed: "Moltmann is left with a finite God who is in the process of developing his own nature. . . Moltmann's God has become basically a limiting concept to hold together the cosmos which is essentially flux or one of open possibility." Larson, "A Review," p. 103.

[19]Moltmann, *Theology of Hope*, pp. 262, 286-289.

[20]Ibid., p. 18.

[21]Ibid., p. 19. Moltmann disparagingly quoted *Christianity Today* when it stated: ". . . man's problem lies in his sins against the Creator, not in domination by capitalistic economic forces." He emphasized that sin is manifested in misery caused by political, social and natural forces. Jurgen Moltmann, *Religion, Revolution, and the Future* (New York: Scribner's Sons, 1969), p. 78.

[22]Moltmann, *Theology of Hope*, p. 20.

[23]Ibid., p. 287.

[24]Larson, "A Review," p. 104.

[25]Moltmann, *Theology of Hope*, p. 284.

[26]Ibid., p. 285.

[27]Ibid., p. 288.

[28]Kee, *Reader*, p. 42.

[29]Harvey Cox, *The Secular City* (New York: MacMillan & Co., 1966), p. 125.

[30]This phrase crops up again and is significant in the thought of those who advocated contextualism.

[31]Kee, *Reader*, p. 52. See Appendix A, p. 79, for the seven theses, of which this quote is the second.

[32]Ibid.

[33]Merle d'Aubigné in his book *History of the Great Reformation* (1840), recounts the direction the Reformers took and fostered among their followers:

> . . . the bond that unites to Christ will be everything to the believing soul. . . Thus, as the doctrine of the Bible had impelled Luther's contemporaries toward Jesus Christ, their love for Jesus Christ, in its turn, impelled them toward the Bible. It was not, as some in our day supposed, from a philosophical necessity or from doubt, or a spirit of inquiry that they reverted to Scripture, it was because they found *there* the words of Him they loved. "You have preached Christ," they said to the Reformer, "let us now hear him *himself*." And they caught at the sheets given to the world as a letter coming to them from heaven.

Quoted in Arthur P. Johnston, "The Bible and World Evangelization," *Trinity World Forum* 2 (1976):2.

[34]Moltmann in Kee, *Reader*, p. 55.

[35]Ibid., p. 67.

[36]Ibid., p. 70. This dialectical methodology also came to be a key aspect in the methodology for contextualizing theology.

[37]Okot P'Bitek, "African Religions in an African University." University of Nairobi, 2 March 1970 (mimeographed), p. 9.

[38]Nissiotis in Kee, *Reader*, p. 82.

[39]Paul Löffler, "The Sources of a Christian Theology of Development," in Kee, *Reader*, p. 77.

[40]Ibid., p. 78. See Chapter 1, above, on the 1971 consultation on "Dogmatic or Contextual Theology?" pp. 4-12.

[41]Avery Dulles, *Review of "A Theology of Liberation,"* by *Gustavo Gutierrez* (Maryknoll, N.Y.: Orbis Books, 1973) excerpted on back of jacket cover.

[42]Ibid.

[43]Gustavo Gutierrez, *A Theology of Liberation* (Maryknoll, N.Y.: Orbis Books, 1973), p. 36.

[44]Ibid., p. 26. As this "theology" has developed, one of its considered strengths has been its identification as a Latin American product. Recently Jürgen Moltmann scoffed at the claim. In March of 1976, in an "Open Letter to José Miguez-Bonino," he faulted the liberation theologians for their "severe criticism of western theology and of theology in general" because "then we are told something about Karl Marx and Friedrich Engels, as if they were Latin American discoveries." To Moltmann not only are these ideological sources for European theology utilized by the theologians of liberation, but also the basic insights of the "Theology of Hope" are used. He calls it a case of ideological re-import without anything "really new" instead of what was, he says, the case in African theology, Japanese theology and North American Black theology. Moltmann sees liberation theology presented in Gutierrez' writings as "the continuation and culmination of the European history of freedom. . . an invaluable contribution to European theology. But where is Latin America in it all?" Se Jürgen Moltmann, "An Open Letter to José Miguez-Bonino: Latin American Liberation Theology," *Christianity and Crisis*, 29 March 1976, pp. 57-63.

[45]Miguez-Bonino, *Doing Theology*, p. xxvii.

[46]Ibid., p. 62.

[47]Gutierrez, *Liberation*, p. 3.

[48]*Ministry in Context* will be considered in Chapter 3, below, pp. 33-44.

[49]TEF, *Ministry in Context*, p. 40.

[50]Gutierrez, *Liberation*, p. 8.

[51]Ibid.

[52]Ibid., p. 218.

[53]Ibid., p. 17, n. 23.

[54]Ibid., p. 11.

[55]Ibid.

[56]Howard Dahl. "The Negation of Theology into Praxis," (M.A. thesis, Trinity Evangelical Divinity School, 1977), p. 97. This illustrates the major difference between the theologians of liberation

and Moltmann. For Moltmann, both God and men were involved. For the liberationists, it was basically all men.

[57] C. Peter Wagner, *Latin American Theology--Radical or Evangelical?* (Grand Rapids: Wm. B. Eerdmans Pub. Co., 1970), p. 21.

[58] Ibid.

[59] For an excellent discussion on the acceptability of liberation theology's use of the Exodus motif, and the more justifiably derived themes based thereon, see Dahl, "The Negation," appendix no. 1.

[60] Gutierrez, *Liberation*, p. 11.

[61] Dahl, "The Negation," p. 78.

[62] David Tracy, *Blessed Rage for Order, The New Pluralism in Theology* (New York: Seabury Press, 1975), p. 243. Quoted in Dahl, "The Negation," p. 7. Dahl also comments in the same context: "The unity of theory and practice. . . one of the dominant themes of Marx."

[63] Gutierrez, *Liberation*, p. 255.

[64] Dahl, "The Negation," pp. 76-77.

[65] The black theology is not as directly related to those who developed contextualization of theology guidelines. It is pertinent to this thesis as a whole and thus is included at this point.

[66] Chancellor Williams, *The Destruction of Black Civilization* (Chicago: Third World Press, 1974), p. 264.

[67] Major J. Jones, *Black Awareness: A Theology of Hope* (New York: Abingdon Press, 1971), p. 118.

[68] Clarence Hilliard, "Down With the Honky Christ--Up With the Funky Jesus," *Christianity Today*, 30 January 1976, pp. 6-8.

[69] James O. Buswell III suggests that it was too much hope that caused the blacks to riot in the mid-sixties. Being told they could rise to equality, and being impatient at the slowness of institutional change, the people revolted in the ghetto. The revolt then splashed over into theology. Buswell holds that much of the loudness of black theology can be traced to the culture--the black theologians desiring an equal but distinct theology (or folk religion?) as well.

[70] Evangelicals, the valiant efforts at redefinition by Hilliard notwithstanding, do not seek such an identification. It is not to their credit, however, that such a theology seems *foreign* to oppressed blacks.

[71] John S. Mbiti, "An African Views American Black Theology," *Worldview* 17 (1974):41.

[72]Most evident in his *Black Theology and Black Power* (New York: Seabury Press, 1969).

[73]Ibid., p. 38.

[74]"Black Theology: A Statement of the National Committee of Black Churchmen," produced by the Committee on Theological Prospectus, issued June 13, 1969, at the Interdenominational Theological Center, Atlanta, Georgia, reproduced in E. F. Frazier and C. Eric Lincoln, *The Negro Church in America--The Black Church Since Frazier* (New York: Schocken Books, 1974), pp. 191-193.

[75]Mbiti, "An African Views," p. 41.

[76]Romans 8:2.

[77]Romans 3:9; Galatians 5:1.

[78]Cone, *Black Theology and Black Power*, p. 40.

[79]Cone, *Liberation*, p. 196. It is not quite clear what this black identity was to be. The Yoruba and Camerounian heritage of the original slaves was systematically destroyed as families were separated, practices were forbidden, and tribes were forcibly mixed.

[80]Cone, *Black Power*, p. 190.

[81]Ibid., p. 191. Thus a white theologian being out of the sphere is judged incapable of making valid judgments on the character of sin.

[82]Cone, *Black Power*, p. 35. Such is true salvation--if sin be only the chains that oppress and bind us in the ghostly way.

[83]Cone, *Liberation*, pp. 186-187.

[84]Of the three basic theories of the atonement, penal, mystical, and classic, Cone and Barth incorporate the latter into their systems. As Barth describes the cosmic duel, a victor-takes-the-spoils motif, and the illusory Satanic afterglow, so Cone sees Christ as in conflict with Satan, in principle. He agreed with Malcolm X that white man is, during this "now," "the devil," and that the "white" structure of this American society, personified in every racist, must be at least part of what the New Testament meant by demonic forces. See Cone, *Black Power*, pp. 40-43.

[85]Ibid., p. 125.

[86]Ibid., p. 126.

[87]His view on Israel is faulty, as he, for example, principlizes too generally from an historical specific instance. This view reinforces his misuse of the biblical text. See Cone, *Black Power*, p. 126.

[88]Ibid.

[89]Discussed in Chapter 1, above, pp. 4-12.

CHAPTER 3

[1]Bishop Karekin Sarkissian, Foreword to *Ministry in Context*, by TEF.

[2]Ibid.

[3]Ibid.

[4]In further references "the committee" will be referred to only by its parent agency, the TEF.

[5]Ibid.

[6]Ibid., Preface.

[7]Ibid., p. 14.

[8]Ibid., p. 13.

[9]Ibid.

[10]Ibid., p. 14.

[11]Ibid.

[12]Ibid., p. 30.

[13]Ibid., p. 14.

[14]Ibid., p. 15.

[15]Ibid., p. 16.

[16]Such thoughts are trapped in a Humean closed universe, surrounded by Kantian scepticism. A combination of both propositional and encounter theology (the evangelical views) seems nearer to the truth. Ronald H. Nash, "Truth by Any Other Name," *Christianity Today*, 7 October 1977, pp. 15-23.

[17]See Appendix B for the text of the policy.

[18]TEF, *Ministry in Context*, p. 18.

[19]Ibid., p. 19.

[20]Ibid., p. 20.

[21]Byang Kato, "The Gospel, Cultural Context and Religious Syncretism," in *Let the Earth Hear His Voice*, ed. J. D. Douglas (Minneapolis: World Wide Publications, 1975), p. 1217. Most evangelical writers examined by this writer thought so too.

[22]Stephen Knapp, "Contextualization and Its Implications for U.S. Evangelical Churches and Mission," Paper delivered at the Missionary Study Fellowship of the Institute of Mennonite Studies, Elkhart, Ind., 5 March 1976, p. 5.

[23]This will be discussed in Chapter 4, below, pp. 52-54.

[24]In an eight page article on context and syncretism, Kato spent approximately one page on contextualization, and five pages on religious syncretism. Kato, "The Gospel," pp. 1216-1223.

[25]See the discussion in Chapter 4, below, pp. 52-76.

[26]Uniformity was not assumed however. Variations of the theme were reasons why each local context was so significant. See TEF, *Ministry in Context*, p. 19, Sections I. 2,3.

[27]Ibid., pp. 18-19, Section I. 1.

[28]Ibid., p. 20.

[29]Ibid., p. 21.

[30]Approach and content were linked in the discussion of this area. Ibid., p. 18.

[31]These would all result from the synthesis. For insight into the interrelatedness see Figure 4 in Chapter 4, below, p. 60.

[32]Ibid., p. 40. An extremely objectionable quote from James Goff of Cuernevaca in *Risk* 7 (1971):32-36 is included in the text of this section of *Ministry in Context*, pp. 40-41.

[33]And yet such seems to have been done in the EFMA '75 discussion summary, EFMA, "Reports," pp. 53-54. The evangelical theories in apparent unawareness of their conceptual (and spiritual) incompatibilities. Note comments on theological "minimum" and "theology of liberation."

[34]Koyama, *Waterbuffalo Theology*, p. 21.

[35]TEF, *Ministry in Context*, p. 19.

[36]Knapp, "Contextualization," p. 5.

[37]Ibid.

[38]Knapp, "Contextualization," p. 5.

[39]TEF, *Ministry in Context*, p. 20.

[40]Ibid.

[41]TEF, *Ministry in Context*, p. 30.

[42]TEF, *Ministry in Context*, pp. 21-25.

[43]Ibid., p. 42. This, of course, is in contrast to the evangelical approach which is historical-grammatical.

[44]Ibid.

[45]This section also encouraged "efforts in consistent dialogue with living faiths and ideologies. . . " a thrust worthy of further evaluation but such is beyond the scope of this book except to note this emphasis in figures 4 and 5 in Chapter 4, below, p. 60.

[46]TEF, *Ministry in Context*, p. 31.

[47]Ibid., p. 47.

[48]Paul Löffler, "The Sources of a Christian Theology of Development," in *In Search of a Theology of Development*, A SODEPAX Report (Geneva: WCC, 1961), pp. 65-73.

[49]For a longer excerpt of the same passage see above, p. 21. As observed above, the insights of neo-orthodoxy appear to have strengthened (or initiated?) the methodology of technical contextualization. Knapp traced this to the epistemological shift noted above, p. 21.

> The TEF documents are perhaps not explicit or
> unanimous enough in calling for this epistemo-
> logical revolution [the reference is to Miquez-
> Bonino's comment: 'There is. . . no knowledge
> except in action itself, in the process of trans-
> forming the world through participation in his-
> tory'] to warrant the conclusion that this call
> in its most radical form is an integral component
> of what the TEF means by 'contextualization.'
> The theology of liberation (in some of its forms)
> as a celebrated example of contextual theology
> is certainly *the most expressive* [emphasis mine]
> at this particular point. But it would appear
> that Shoki Coe and Aharon Sapsezian, two of the
> TEF directors, see this kind of a challenge to
> traditional epistemology as *at least implicit* in
> authentic contextualization in any context.

Knapp, "Contextualization," p. 9.

[50]This is how many popular contextualizers appear to have acted. This term is defined below, pp. 47-51.

[51]Maurus Heinrichs might further exemplify another facet of this base. To him there were many, perhaps even too many, doctrines that qualified as *de fide definita*. In his paper on Roman Catholic accommodation/contextualization he wrote: "One should never forget that these systems are basically not anti-Christian but pre-

Christian, and in principle were formed under the economy of salvation. Though they are ways from below, they are not without the influence of God." "Cultural and Temporal Perspectives in Presenting the Faith," *Teaching All Nations* (Manila) 4 (1967):144.

[52]Those who shared an ideological base with TEF automatically fell into this group. This term has been coined by this author.

[53]The Secretariat: Theology in the Americas, "Contextualization of North American Theology," (New York: Theology in the Americas, [1976]), pp. 1-12, and The Secretariat: Theology in the Americas, "The Theology in the Americas Process," (New York: Theology in the Americas, [1976]), pp. 1-8.

[54]Theology in the Americas, "Contextualization," p. 1.

[55]Ibid.

[56]Ibid., p. 4.

[57]Ibid., pp 4-5.

[58]Ibid., p. 5.

[59]Ibid., p. 4.

[60]Theology in the Americas, "Process," p. 1.

[61]Ibid., p. 3.

[62]Ibid., p. 6.

[63]Ibid.

[64]Ibid., p. 5.

[65]Ibid.

[66]Ibid., p. 4.

[67]Ibid., p. 1.

[68]Theology in the Americas, "Contextualization," p. 3.

[69]Ibid., p. 2.

[70]Theology in the Americas, "Process," p. 5.

[71]Theology in the Americas, "Contextualization," p. 5.

[72]Ibid., p. 3.

[73]Ibid., p. 11.

[74]Ibid.

[75] Ibid.

[76] The term has been coined by this writer.

[77] For more on this parallel see Chapter 4, below, pp. 58-61.

[78] For more on this term which has been coined by the writer, see Chapter 4, below, pp. 67-76.

[79] See the author's Thesis wherein several chapters show that John S. Mbiti may serve as a prime example of a popular contextualizer. Bruce C. E. Fleming, *Contextualization of Theology as Evidenced in Africa in the Writings of John Samuel Mbiti* (Deerfield, Ill.: Trinity Evangelical Divinity School, 1977), pp. 119-184.

[80] From 1966 to 1972.

[81] *Waterbuffalo Theology* (Maryknoll, N.Y.: Orbis Books, 1974).

[82] Ibid., p. 20.

[83] Ibid.

[84] TEF, *Ministry in Context*, p. 20.

[85] *Waterbuffalo Theology*, p. 21. This last comment is the same basic assessment as given by Knapp quoted above, p. 40.

[86] Ibid., p. 23. Of the two persons discussed in this section on popular contextualization, Koyama is near to the TEF end of the continuum, and Von Allmen is nearer the evangelical end of the continuum.

[87] Ibid., p. 24. Lynn A. DeSilva seems to have found in Sri Lanka what Koyama seeks to foster. He has written: "As a result of these efforts there is now emerging an indigenous expression of the Christian faith based on a theological structure oriented to the conceptual framework of Buddhism." "Theological Construction in a Buddhist Context," in J. N. D. Anderson, ed., *Asian Voices in Christian Theology* Maryknoll, N.Y.: Orbis Books, 1976), p. 40.

[88] To this observer.

[89] Worthy of note in light of this discussion are his chapters seven and thirteen: "Aristotelian Pepper and Buddhist Salt" and "Cool *Arahant* and Hot God." Also interesting is his concept of "innocent secularism." It is considered "innocent" because to Koyama secularism in Thailand is not reacting against the God of history, but is attempting to be active in history for the first time. Secularism as anti-*apatheia* is therefore "for" Christianity with its linear concept of time!

[90] Anderson, *Asian Voice in Christian Theology* also reflects such a disconnected character.

[91]The German heritage of higher criticism shows rather clearly in Koyama's chapter fifteen, "In Search of a 'Personality' of Theology in Asia." (pp. 173-186).   Although placing a commendable emphasis on the cross, he wrongly interprets the Exodus.   Although Abraham went out, he'll be coming back and all will be saved, he thought.

[92]Daniel Von Allmen, "The Birth of Theology: "Contextualization as the dynamic element in the formation of New Testament Theology," *International Review of Mission* 64 (January 1965):37-52.   This article was praised by Gerald H. Anderson.

[93]Ibid., p. 48.

[94]Ibid., p. 49.

[95]With this assessment John Mbiti also was said to agree.   Personal conversation with Prof. Robert Evans, McCormick Theological Seminary, Chicago, August 1976.

[96]Von Allmen, "Birth," p. 39.

[97]Ibid., pp. 39-41.

[98]Ibid., p. 44.

[99]A study of ecumenical conferences such as Bangkok '73 and Nairobi '75 will show that the emphasis on the principles and prejudices of contextualization had not abated.   See for example, *Bangkok Assembly '73* (New York: WCC, 1973), p. 58, and David M. Paton, ed., *Breaking Barriers, Nairobi 1975* (Grand Rapids: Wm. B. Eerdmans, 1976), pp. 198, 251, 260, 305.

CHAPTER 4

[1]TEF, *Ministry in Context*, p. 20.

[2]See Figure 3 above in Chapter 3, p. 49.

[3]EFMA, "Report," pp. 53-54.

[4]Saphir P. Athyal, "Emergence of Asian Theologies," *Christianity Today*, 23 September 1977, p. 72.

[5]Ibid.

[6]Peter Beyerhaus, *Bangkok '73: The Beginning or End of World Mission?* (Grand Rapids: Wm. B. Eerdmans Pub. Co., 1974).

[7]Ibid., p. 22.

[8]Ibid., pp. 22-23.

[9]See Figure 3 above in Chapter 3, p. 49.

[10]Orlando E. Costas, *The Church and Its Mission: A Shattering Critique from the Third World* (Wheaton, Ill.: Tyndale House Pub., 1974).

[11]Selectively represented in this thesis by Augustine, Luther, Calvin, A. H. Strong, Hodge, Pieper, Pinnock, and others.

[12]Peter Berger, *Rumor of Angels* (New York: Doubleday, 1969), p. 98.

[13]Kenneth S. Kantzer, Highland Park, Ill., June 1977. Private telephone conversation with the writer.

[14]Clark H. Pinnock, *Biblical Revelation: The Foundation of Christian Theology* (Chicago: Moody Press, 1971), pp. 114-115.

[15]Charles Hodge, *Systematic Theology*, 3 Vols. (New York: Charles Scribner & Co., 1872), 1:13.

[16]Ibid., p. 3.

[17]A. H. Strong, *Systematic Theology* (Valley Forge, Pa.: Judson Press, 1907), p. 2.

[18]"Authority and Uniqueness of Scripture Report," in *Let the Earth Hear*, ed. J. D. Douglas, p. 994.

[19]L. Gaussen, *Divine Inspiration of the Bible* (Grand Rapids: Kregel Publications, 1971), p. 350. See also B. B. Warfield, *The Inspiration and Authority of the Bible*, ed. Samuel G. Craig (Philadelphia: Presbyterian & Reformed Pub. Co., 1948).

[20]C. H. Dodd, *The Apostolic Preaching and Its Developments* (London: Hodder & Stoughton, 1936).

[21]Pinnock, *Biblical Revelation*, p. 109.

[22]A problem harkening back to the imported theological base.

[23]Donald A. McGavran, "The Biblical Base from which Adjustments are Made," in *Christopaganism or Indigenous Christianity?* (South Pasadena: William Carey Library, 1975), p. 41.

[24]Athyal, "Emergence," p. 72.

[25]Francis Pieper, *Christian Dogmatics*, 3 vols. (St. Louis: Concordia Pub. House, 1950), 1:46.

[26]This fact is recognized by many. And even regenerate experimenters will have difficulty. Athyal acknowledges that

> Asian Christianity, in understanding the Gospel
> in the context of the religions, cultures, and
> philosophical milieu in comtemporary Asia, should
> produce its own creative thinkers and apologists.
> But it seems at the same time to be having its

> share in producing *indigenous heresies* [emphasis
> mine]. This possibly cannot be helped any more
> than it could be helped in the development of
> Western theological systems.

Athyal, "Emergence," p. 72.

[27]Pinnock, *Biblical Theology*, p. 113.

[28]See Figures 1 and 2 above in Chapter 1, p. 9.

[29]J. Deotis Roberts wrote:

> The search for a cosmic Christ has broadened my
> horizon. Christocentrism has not been abated,
> but Christ as giver of grace is seen as author
> of nature and *Lord of history* [emphasis mine] as
> well. The *incarnation* remains the center of God's
> redemptive revelation. The circumference of *reve-*
> *lation*, however, *has been expanded*. . . God's all
> pervasive *revelation*. It is manifest in creation
> and providence and is in all times and among *all*
> peoples.

"Contextual Theology: Liberation and Indigenization," *The Christian
Century*, 28 January 1976, pp. 64-65.

[30]See Figure 4 above, p. 60.

[31]See Figure 5 above, p. 60. Is it fair to push the diagram to
the limits and note how little influence schematically, dogmatics,
and even the Bible as a whole would eventually exert? Biblical
motifs would be emphasized continually to be sure. But imbalance
between the biblical and the contextual seems highly likely.

[32]Arthur P. Johnston, "Focus on the Bible and World Evangelization," *Trinity World Forum* 2 (Fall 1976):1-3.

[33]Ibid. It is often assumed that contextualization, evangelical
style, would occur at level six only. For justification of the
above statements and for a chart adapted to context-indigenization
see below, Figure 8, p. 75.

[34]It might be suggested that *all* levels, 1-6, would be affected.

[35]In his paper "Should the Church Still Talk about Salvation?"
included in the preparatory study material for the Bangkok Conference of the CWME, George Johnson wrote:

> . . . the Church may well hesitate to stress in
> liturgy or doctrine the *key* concept [emphasis
> mine] of Paul. 'I have complete confidence in
> the gospel: it is God's power to save all who be-
> lieve. . . ' (Romans 1:16). This vogue is de-
> based if not outworn; the words do not speak to
> one's condition.

In Beyerhaus, *Bangkok '73*, p. 122.

[36]Lausanne participants sounded a distinctly different call. In the Covenant they stated:

> . . . evangelism itself is the proclamation of the historical, biblical Christ as Savior and Lord, with a view to *persuading people* [emphasis mine] to come to him personally and so be reconciled to God. . . and identify themselves with his new community. The results of evangelism include obedience to Christ, *incorporation into his church* and responsible service in the world.

"The Lausanne Covenant," in *Let the Earth Hear*, ed. J. D. Douglas, p. 4.

[37]This is closely related to the belief in universal salvation and the search for the cosmic Christ.

[38]Classic examples of the former are Nevius, *Planting and Development of Missionary Churches*, and Melvin Hodges, *A Guide to Church Planting* (Chicago: Moody Press, 1973).

[39]Exemplified in Donald McGavran, *The Clash*, pp. 1-10.

[40]George Peters, "The Relationship of Christianity to Non-Christian Cultures," [c. 1976] p. 2, (mimeographed).

[41]See especially volume one of the two volume set compiled by Francis Wayland of the *Memoirs of Rev. Dr. Judson* (Boston: Phillips, Sampson, & Co., 1853).

[42]Some changes in the cultures were unabashedly advocated by missionaries on the scene. An interesting study is James S. Dennis, *Christian Missions and Social Progress: A Sociological Study of Foreign Missions*, 3 vols. (London: Oliphant Anderson & Ferrier, 1899). Various cultural phenomena were labeled as "social evils of the non-Christian world" and vigorously attacked. These resulted in significant changes in local culture and included abolition of the slave trade, suttee and footbinding, and establishment of orphanages (with children in western dress), hospitals, and vocational training centers.

[43]Even marketing research has entered the field. See H. Wilbert Norton and James F. Engel, *What's Gone Wrong with the Harvest?: A Communication Strategy for the Church and World Evangelization* (Grand Rapids: Zondervan Pub. House, 1975).

[44]Jacob A. Loewen, *Culture and Human Values: Christian Intervention in Anthropological Perspective* (South Pasadena: William Carey Library, 1975), pp. xi-xii.

[45]Kato, "The Gospel," p. 1217.

[46]Ibid., p. 1003.

[47]Ibid.

[48]Taken from personal discussions, Deerfield, Ill., March 1976.

[49]Kato, "The Gospel," p. 1217. Note again his watchfulness against heresy. Perhaps this discussion is begging the questions, "Just what cultural clothes of Bible times are removed and what new ones are added? And what is that core to be communicated first, that is undressed and dressed again?" These are very real and legitimate questions. Matters of intent, content and context are knotty ones and must not be overlooked. See further the discussion section report on Kato's paper at Lausanne, "The Gospel, Contextualization and Syncretism Report" by Bradshaw and Savage, in *Let the Earth Hear*, ed. J. D. Douglas, pp. 1224-1228, and the area reports which give more detailed examples, pp. 1229-1293. For more of the basic categories in such a discussion see Howard W. Law, *Winning a Hearing: An Introduction to Anthropology and Linguistics* (Grand Rapids: Wm. B. Eerdmans Pub. Co., 1968).

[50]For exemplary evangelical works in this rich area see especially Bernard Ramm et al., *Hermeneutics* (Grand Rapids: Baker Book House, 1971), and Carl F. H. Henry, ed., *Revelation and the Bible* (Grand Rapids: Baker Book House, 1959).

[51]H. Richard Niebuhr, *Christ and Culture* (New York: Harper & Row, Publishers, 1951).

[52]"A Preliminary Format for a Comprehensive Bibliography on the 'Contextualization' of the Gospel," (Typewritten). Other comments in this thesis on Niebuhr's systematization closely follow this outline.

[53]Ibid.

[54]Louis J. Luzbetak, *The Church and Culture* (Techny, Ill.: Divine Word Publications, 1970).

[55]The William S. Carter Symposium of 1974 held at Milligan College and reproduced in book form as *Christopaganism or Indigenous Christianity?* assessed the accommodation-syncretism axis from various angles.

[56]Eugene Nida has done outstanding work in this area.

[57]John S. Mbiti has been especially vocal in this legitimate call. Note the list given by Idowu mentioned in Chapter 1, above, p.3.

[58]In this day of nationalism practically all people are demanding the right to be "at home" in all areas, including at church, in business, in industry and in politics.

[59]Reprinted in J. Herbert Kane, *A Global View of Christian Missions* (Grand Rapids: Baker Book House, 1971), p. 266. See his index, p. 583 for his references to outstanding indigenous churches.

[60]Jahnheinz Jahn, *Muntu* (London: Faber, 1961).

[61]Some theologians, John Mbiti included, are suspicious of "making" anything local "indigenous." "The church is made up of individuals from the locality. Can one make them any more indigenous?" they ask. Under discussion here, however, is the process of letting the gospel move into all areas and even nooks and crannies of a given culture, to shed light everywhere.

[62]See Appendix B.

[63]James O. Buswell III. Discussion with this writer on evangelical vs. non-evangelical indigenization, Wheaton, Ill., October 1977.

[64]James O. Buswell III, "Contextualization: Theory, Tradition, and Method," a paper presented at the Trinity Consultation on Theology and Missions, Deerfield, Ill., 22-25 March 1976, pp. 4-16.

[65]Ibid.

[66]For example, Peter Savage suggested, in "Discipleship in Context: The Challenge of 'Contextualization,'" (mimeographed), pp. 1-2, a twofold division (1) the missiological thrust or indigenization and (2) the pastoral thrust, or reformation. His subunits under "indigenization" are confusing, however, and include items from all three of Buswell's categories. Worthy of note is that Savage advocates the Christ-against-culture position.

[67]This is Buswell's description of Barney's term, Buswell, "Contextualization," p. 5. One might suggest a more precise phrasing equating the gospel with the transcultural.

[68]Or archetypal theology.

[69]Or ectypal theology.

[70]Private conversation with the writer, Deerfield, Ill., May 1976.

[71]The terms are consistent with anthropological terminology.

[72]G. Linwood Barney, "The Supracultural and the Cultural: Implications for Frontier Missions," in *The Gospel and Frontier Peoples*, ed. R. Pierce Beaver (South Pasadena: William Carey Library, 1973), p. 51, quoted by Buswell, "Contextualization," pp. 5-6.

[73]Buswell lumped quite a diverse group together. Yet his basic point is true and it may be observed that these people are all in the same ballpark, except, perhaps, some Roman Catholics. Buswell wrote of processes that encompass various parts of the context-indigenization process:

> This is essentially the meaning of Charles Kraft's
> usage of 'transculturation,' of William Wonderley's
> and S. R. Garcia's (and others') usage of 'incarna-
> tion,' of Lusbetak's usage of 'accommodation' and
> Roman Catholics' (and others') general use of 'adap-
> tion.' It is essentially what John Beekmen means
> by 'a culturally relevant witness,' what William D.
> Rayburn means by 'transformed symbolism,' what

> Michael Green, Ralph Winter, and others have
> emphasized with reference to the 'flexibility'
> of the early church witness, and what Nida,
> Kraft, and other translators call 'dynamic
> (functional) equivalence translations.' It is
> what J. Merle Davis meant by the title of his
> anthropologically oriented *New Buildings on
> Old Foundations*. . .

Ibid., p. 6.

[74]Suggested by Buswell in conversation with this writer,
Wheaton, Ill., 7 September 1977.

[75]Preaching and apologetics do not cease after the initial con-
tacts, of course.

[76]Knapp, "Contextualization," p. 21.

[77]See the discussion on the Sawi in Don Richardson's, *Peace Child*
(Glendale, Calif.: Regal Books, 1974).

[78]Herein lies a distinction of context-indigenization from contextualization. The activities of preaching and apologetics are anathema to the conceptualization of truth evidenced by the TEF. In
contextualization, praxis, affirmed by self-validating action, becomes orthopraxis, or relevant truth in action. Revealed Theology
and its understood form, Partial Theology, must be conceptually, as
well as actively, communicated. The "deposit of the faith" must be
transmitted by concept and comparison, preaching point and application, insight and illustration. See Miguez-Bonino's somewhat unfair
but insightful comments on the two epistemological systems, reproduced in Knapp, "Contextualization," p. 9 from Miguez-Bonino, *Doing
Theology*.

[79]G. W. Peters in his paper "Contemporary Practices," p. 181,
wrote:

> . . . a method which may be very effective at one
> time, at one place, among one people, may not be
> effective at another time, another place, another
> people. In fact, it may prove disadvantageous if
> not disastrous. . . We do not need renewal of the
> Gospel, but we do need continuous renewal of method-
> ology to communicate the age-old Gospel in intel-
> ligible, meaningful, and purposeful manner.

[80]G. W. Peters, "Contemporary Practices of Evangelism," in *Let
the Earth Hear*, ed. J. D. Douglas, pp. 195-196.

[81]The varying forms of EID from Latin America to Africa's "New
Life for All" and especially Japan's *"Sodoin Dendo"* implemented cultural adjustment.

[82]This term will be defined in the second section following.

[83]Consider the condemnation of those who worshipped Molech, regardless of how sincere or "ethnic" they might have been in their worship. Leviticus 18:21; 20:2-5; I Kings 11:7, etc.

[84]Knapp, "Contextualization," p. 15.

[85]See Comments on the "three-self emphasis" above, p. 65.

[86]Buswell strongly takes issue with the TEF's desire to move beyond indigenization, condemning it as past-centered and static. He writes: "In the first place, there is nothing necessarily static about the concept. Its etymology involves Latin morphemes meaning 'to bear or produce within.'" "Contextualization," p. 10.

[87]Ibid.

[88]Matthew 5:13-16.

[89]AEAM, "A.E.A.M. Declaration on the Christian Family," *Afroscope*, October 1977, pp. 5-7.

[90]Charles H. Kraft, "Dynamic Equivalence Churches: An Ethnotheological Approach to Indigeneity," *Missiology* 1 (January 1973): 56, cited by Buswell, "Contextualization," p. 14.

[91]Ibid.

[92]Knapp, "Contextualization," p. 7.

[93]Knapp anticipated such an evaluation and tried to show the incorrectness of it. His reasoning seems faulty on this point, however.

[94]John Mbiti took special note of time sequence among the Akamba. Knapp evaluated his work:

> Mbiti's challenge to Cullmann about the imposition of Greek views of time onto the biblical data in the latter's biblical theology is an example of the kind of multi-cultural interaction that can contribute significantly to a clearer grasp of biblical theology progressively freed from enslavement to post-Biblical cultural perspectives.

Knapp, "Contextualization," p. 33.

[95]Ibid., p. 16.

[96]Charles H. Kraft, "Toward a Christian Ethnotheology," in *God, Man and Church Growth*, ed. A. R. Tippett (Grand Rapids: Wm. B. Eerdmans Pub. Co., 1973), p. 110.

[97]James O. Buswell III, "Ethnocentrism and a Theology of Crisis," *Trinity World Forum* 1 (Fall 1975):5.

[98]The most obvious of these in the realm of *missiology* are the death and resurrection of Christ, the Great Commission, and the infilling and enabling power of the mission-minded Holy Spirit.

[99]James Orr's famous lecture series of 1897 on *The Progress of Dogma* published under that title (Grand Rapids: Wm. B. Eerdmans Pub. Co., 1952) provided the classic outlines of the development of doctrine that basically have been accepted transculturally. They were developed in the various ages of the church: (1) The second century --the age of *apologetics* and vindication of *fundamental ideas of religion*. (2) The third and fourth centuries--the period of the *theological* controversies (doctrine of God). (3) The beginning of the fifth century--the period of *anthropological* period (doctrine of Atonement). (6) The sixteenth century--the period of controversies on the *application of redemption* (Justification, etc.). (7) The recent centuries--on *Eschatology*. To Orr's list perhaps the concern for the *Holy Spirit* (Pneumatological) and concern for the nature and extent of *Revelation* could be added as the concern for modern times.

[100]This would relate to the "sameness" of all men as has been illustrated in research. See in Kraft, "Ethnotheology," p. 123. This drawing of universals can be used to justify to some extent the drawing of universals done by John Mbiti especially in his book *Concepts of God in Africa*.

[101]Such as organizing doctrines around the theme of power politics between angels and demons, sinners and righteous, the church and the world and so forth. Thus extra chapters would be written. Others would be rewritten and perhaps corrected or expanded.

[102]Knapp wrote: "Renewing, transforming, and at times rejecting the culture which surrounds it and of which it partakes is of the essence of the church. . . The responsibility of the church is to be subject to Christ's Lordship in its very existence which at every point involves the utilization, transformation, or rejection of culture." "Contextualization," p. 19. See also Ephesians 6:12.

[103]Isaiah 59:1-14, 16a.

APPENDIX A

[1]Alistair Kee, ed. *A Reader in Political Theology* (Philadelphia: Westminster Press, 1974). pp. 51-57.

Bibliography

BOOKS ON CONTEXTUALIZATION AND RELATED DISCIPLINES

Anderson, Gerald H., ed. *Asian Voices in Christian Theology*. Maryknoll, N.Y.: Orbis Books, 1976.

Anderson, Gerald H. and Stransky, Thomas F., ed. *Mission Trends No. 2*. New York: Paulist Press; Grand Rapids: Wm. B. Eerdmans Pub. Co., 1975.

Beyerhaus, Peter. *Bangkok '73: The Beginning or End of World Mission?* Grand Rapids: Zondervan Publishing House, 1974.

Cone, James H. *Black Theology and Black Power*. New York: Seabury Press, 1969.

_____. *A Black Theology of Liberation*. Philadelphia: Lippincott, 1970.

Costas, Orlando E. *The Church and Its Mission: A Shattering Critique from the Third World*. Wheaton, Ill.: Tyndale House Pub., 1974.

Dahl, Howard. "The Negation of Theology into Praxis." M.A. thesis, Trinity Evangelical Divinity School, 1977.

Douglas, J. D., ed. *Let the Earth Hear His Voice: International Congress on World Evangelization, Lausanne, Switzerland*. Minneapolis: World Wide Publication, 1975

Gundry, Stanley N.; and Johnson, Alan F., ed. *Tensions in Contemporary Theology*. Chicago: Moody Press, 1976.

Gutierrez, Gustavo. *A Theology of Liberation*. Maryknoll, N.Y.: Orbis Books, 1973.

Idowu, E. Bolaji. *Towards an Indigenous Church*. Ibadan: Oxford University Press, 1965.

Kee, Alistair, ed. *A Reader in Political Theology*. Philadelphia: Westminster Press, 1974.

Koyama, Kosuke. *Waterbuffalo Theology*. Maryknoll, N.Y.: Orbis Books, 1974.

Lusbetak, Louis J. *The Church and Cultures: An Applied Anthropology for the Religious Worker*. Techny, Ill.: Divine Word Pubs., 1970.

Mayers, Marvin K. *Christianity Confronts Culture: A Strategy for Cross-Cultural Evangelism*. Grand Rapids: Zondervan Publishing House, 1974.

Miguez-Bonino, José. *Doing Theology in a Revolutionary Situation*. Philadelphia: Fortress Press, 1975.

Moltmann, Jürgen. *Religion, Revolution, and the Future*. New York: Scribner's Sons, 1969.

_____. *Theology of Hope*. Evanston: Harper & Row, 1967.

Nida, Eugene. *Religion Across Cultures: A study in the communication of Christian faith*. New York: Harper & Row, 1967.

Nevius, John L. *Planting and Development of Missionary Churches*. 4th ed. Philadelphia: Presbyterian & Reformed Pub. Co., 1958.

Niebuhr, H. Richard. *Christ and Culture*. New York: Harper & Row, 1951.

Orr, James. *The Progress of Dogma*. Grand Rapids: Wm. B. Eerdmans Pub. Co., 1952.

Pobee, John S. *Religion in a Pluralistic Society: Essays Presented to Professor C. G. Baeta*. Leiden: E. J. Brill, 1976.

Richardson, Don. *Peace Child*. Glendale, Calif.: Regal Books, 1974.

Robinson, Richard C. "An Examination of an African Philosophical World View with Reference to Traditional Religion." M.A. thesis, Trinity Evangelical Divinity School, 1977.

Theological Education Fund. *Ministry in Context: The Third Mandate Programme of the Theological Education Fund (1970-77)*. Bromley, Kent, United Kingdom: New Life Press, 1972.

Yamamori, Tetsunao; and Taber, Charles R., ed. *Christopaganism or Indigenous Christianity?* South Pasadena, Cal.: William Carey Library, 1975.

ARTICLES ON CONTEXTUALIZATION AND RELATED DISCIPLINES

"Annotated List of Periodicals Concerned with the Vocation, Role and Function of Christianity in Africa, Asia and Latin America." *Exchange.* (Leiden) 1 (1972):1-24.

Athyal, Saphir P. "Emergence of Asian Theologies." *Christianity Today*, 23 September 1977, pp. 72-73.

Buswell, James O. III. "Contextualization: Theory, Tradition, and Method." Paper presented at the Trinity Consultation on Theology and Missions, Deerfield, Ill., 22-25 March 1976, pp. 4-16.

_____. "Ethnocentrism and a Theology of Crisis." *Trinity World Forum* 1 (Fall 1975):5.

Campbell, Richard. "Contextual Theology and Its Problems." *Study Encounter* 12 (1976):11-25.

Coe, Shoki. "Authentic contextuality leads to contextualization." *Theological Education* 9 (Summer 1973):24-25.

Conn, Harvie M. "Contextualization: A New Dimension for Cross-Cultural Hermeneutic." *Evangelical Missions Quarterly* 14 (January 1978):39-46.

Droogers, André. "The Africanization of Christianity: An Anthropologist's View." *Missiology* 5 (October 1972): 443-456.

Heinrichs, Maurus. "Cultural Perspectives in Presenting the Faith." *Teaching All Nations* 4 (1967):327-339.

_____. "An Attempt at a Systematic Theology Along Eastern Lines of Thought." *Teaching All Nations* 4 (1967):327-339.

Hodges, Melvin L. "Are indigenous church principles outdated?" *Evangelical Missions Quarterly* 9 (Fall 1972):43-46.

Johnston, Arthur P. "Revolution, Liberation Theology and Indigenization of Theology." n.p. [1975] (mimeographed).

_____. "The Bible and World Evangelization." *Trinity World Forum* 2 (Fall 1976):1-3.

Kinsler, F. Ross. "Mission and Context: The Current Debate About Contextualization." *Evangelical Missions Quarterly* 14 (January 1978): 23-29.

Knapp, Stephen C. "Contextualization and Its Implications for U.S. Evangelical Churches and Missions." Paper delivered at the Missionary Study Fellowship of the Institute of Mennonite Studies, Elkhart, Ind., 5 March 1976.

Kraft, Charles H. "God's model for cross-cultural communication—the incarnation." *Evangelical Missions Quarterly* 9 (Summer 1973):205-216.

_____. "The Contextualization of Theology." *Evangelical Missions Quarterly* 14 (January 1978):31-36.

Larson, Christopher. "*Theology of Hope*: A Review." *Trinity Studies* 2 (1972):103-108.

Mbiti, John S. "An African Views—American Black Theology." *Worldview* 17 (August 1974):41-44.

McDonald, H. Dermot. "The Lusts of Modern Theology." *Christianity Today*, 21 October 1977, pp. 84-86.

Muller-Kruger, Theodor. "The Cultural Orientation of Theological Education." *South East Asia Journal of Theology* 6 (1965): 59-73.

Nash, Ronald H. "Truth by Any Other Name," *Christianity Today*, 7 October 1977, pp. 15-23.

Nicholls, Bruce. "Toward an Asian Theology of Mission." *Evangelical Mission Quarterly* 6 (1970):65-78.

Nida, Eugene A. "Christo-Paganism." *Practical Anthropology* 8 (1961): 1-15.

Nunez, Emilio A. "Contextualization: Latin American Theology." *1975 Mission Executives Retreat Report-EFMA*. Washington, D.C.: n.p., 1975.

Padilla, C. Rene. "The Contextualization of the Gospel: A learning in dialogue experience produced by Partnership in Mission." Presented at Pinebrook, Stroudsburg, Pa., June 1975.

Ro, Bong Rin. "Contextualization: Asian Theology." *1975 Mission Executives Retreat Report--EFMA*. Washington, D.C.: n.p., 1975.

Roberts, J. Deotis, Sr. "Contextual Theology: Liberation and Indigenization." *Christian Century*, 25 January 1976, pp. 64-68.

Robinson, John F. "Contextualization and African Theology." *1975 Mission Executives Retreat Report--EFMA*. Washington, D. C.: n.p., 1975.

Rossman, Vern. "The Breaking in of the Future. The Problem of Indigenous and Cultural Synthesis." *International Review of Missions* 52 (1963):129-143; 191-194.

Rowen, Samuel F. "About This Issue." *Evangelical Missions Quarterly* 14 (January 1978):2-3.

Savage, Peter. "Discipleship in Context: The Challenge of 'Contex-
    tualization.'" Contextualization Study Group. Abingdon: Partner-
    ship in Mission, 29-31 January 1976 (Mimeographed).

Stompul, A. A., ed. "Theological Education within the Whole People
    of God: International consultation on theological education held
    at the Ecumenical Institute Chateau Bossey, 21-27 September 1975."
    Geneva: Lutheran World Federation Department of Church Coopera-
    tion and Department of Studies.

Stompul, A. A. and Rajaratnam, K., ed. "Theological Education in
    Today's Asia: Theological education and training for witness and
    service, held in Manila, Philippines, 21-24 October 1976)."
    Geneva: Lutheran World Federation Department of Church Coopera-
    tion and Department of Studies.

Theology in the Americas, The Secretariat. "Contextualization of
    North American Theology." New York: Theology of the Americas,
    1976, pp. 1-12.

_____. "The Theology in the Americas Process," New York: Theol-
    ogy in the Americas, 1976, pp. 1-8.

Von Allmen, Daniel. "The Birth of Theology: Contextualization as the
    dynamic element in the formulation of New Testament theology."
    International Review of Mission 64 (January 1975):37-55.

Indexes

SELECTED NAMES

SIGNIFICANT CONCEPTS AND TERMS

SELECTED ORGANIZATIONS, PUBLICATIONS, PLACES

Bruce Fleming

Bruce Fleming is a missionary of the Evangelical Free Church of America. Both he and his wife, Joy Elasky Fleming, are involved in theological education in Francophone Africa. He has received the degrees of Master of Divinity in Missions and Master of Theology in Missions and Evangelism from Trinity Evangelical Divinity School in Deerfield, Illinois.